BUREAU OF LAND MANAGEMENT

Back Country
Byways

By STEWART M. GREEN

With a foreword by CY JAMISON

Director of the Bureau of Land Management

FALCON PRESS®

Recreation Guides from Falcon Press
The Angler's Guide to Montana
The Hiker's Guide to Colorado
The Beartooth Fishing Guide
The Hiker's Guide to Idaho
The Floater's Guide to Colorado
The Hiker's Guide to Utah
The Hiker's Guide to Arizona
The Hiker's Guide to Washington
The Hiker's Guide to California
The Hiker's Guide to Nevada
The Hunter's Guide to Montana
The Rockhound's Guide to Montana
The Hiker's Guide to Montana's Continental Divide Trail
The Hiker's Guide to Hot Springs in the Pacific Northwest
Recreation Guide to California National Forests
Hiker's Guide to New Mexico

Falcon Press is continually expanding its list of recreational guidebooks using the same general format as this book. All books include detailed descriptions, accurate maps, and all information necessary for enjoyable trips. You can order extra copies of this book and get information and prices for the books listed above by writing Falcon Press, P.O. Box 1718, Helena, MT 59624. Also, please ask for a free copy of our current catalog listing all Falcon Press books.

Library of Congress Catalog Card Number: 91-070769
ISBN: 1-56044-061-9
Manufactured in the United States of America.

Falcon Press Publishing Co., Inc.
P.O. Box 1718, Helena, MT 59624

All photos by the author.
Back Cover Photos: L-Stewart Green on Alpine Loop Byway. R-Cliff Leight on Nine Mile Canyon Byway.
Cover Photo: Stewart Green on Gold Belt Byway.

ACKNOWLEDGMENTS

Every book has a beginning. *Back Country Byways* began with a phone call from Falcon Press publisher Bill Schneider on a gray March day. Seven months later I drove the Fort Meade Byway, my last byway journey, on another gray day that dropped a foot of snow on the Black Hills. In between I traveled over 16,000 miles in eleven western states, camped out for forty-three nights, replaced a muffler in Medford, Oregon, broke a piston in my Bronco on Utah's Henry Mountains, and filled a file cabinet drawer with notes, maps, brochures, and other Back Country Byways material.

Thanks to everyone who had a hand in making this book. The BLM's district and area managers and outdoor recreation planners provided answers to my questions about their byways. They graciously reviewed and commented on the manuscripts and maps to ensure accuracy. They took time out from busy schedules to meet with me or drive me on the byway in their district.

Many thanks to Bill Schneider, publisher of Falcon Press, for the opportunity to travel, write, and photograph our Back Country Byway system. Thanks also to Falcon's Malcolm Bates for editing the book.

Lastly, thanks to my family—Nancy, Ian, and Brett—for their support, patience, and encouragement. This book also belongs to them. They shared my campfires, starry nights, desert storms, and byway adventures.

"For my part, I travel not to go anywhere, but to go.
I travel for travel's sake. The great affair is to move."

—Robert Louis Stevenson
Travels With a Donkey, 1879

CONTENTS

OREGON

SOUTH DAKOTA

UTAH

WYOMING

FOREWORD

Today with the bustle of airports, train stations and crowded interstates, travel for the average American is anything but enjoyable. We of the Department of the Interior's Bureau of Land Management (BLM) are trying to change all that with a new program in the West called Back Country Byways. Back Country Byways combine America's century-old love affair with motor vehicles and the outdoors. The program is aimed at providing the public with recreational driving opportunities while informing them about natural and cultural resources and multiple use activities on the nation's public lands.

The program is the BLM's unique contribution to the larger National Scenic Byways program, generally associated with our sister agency, the United States Forest Service. Both are the result of a 1987 study by the President's Commission on Americans Outdoors that found that forty-three percent of American adults identified driving for pleasure as a favorite pastime.

The BLM administers the nation's largest land system—and also the least explored. Currently, nearly forty-four byways have been identified in eleven states totaling almost 2,000 miles. Recreational visits to the BLM lands are around sixty million a year and are increasing at a rate of two million visits annually. We plan to identify another forty to fifty routes in the next two to three years.

The Back Country Byways program relies on partnerships with state and local governments and the private sector. We are working in cooperation with these groups and organizations to provide interpretive materials about our byways. And the many people who use the byways support the program by caring for the environment and the many resources along the way.

I invite you to enjoy America's Back Country Byways and to see the variety and richness of the nation's public lands.

Cy Jamison, Director
Bureau of Land Management, Department of the Interior

PARTNERS IN BACK COUNTRY BYWAYS

The Bureau of Land Management's Back Country Byways program has many friends. Chief among them is the American Recreation Coalition (ARC), a non-profit Washington-based federation whose membership consists of more than 100 recreation associations and corporations. One of ARC's primary missions has been the stimulation of partnerships to provide quality recreation opportunities.

For the Back Country Byways program, ARC enlisted the support of three corporations: Farmers Insurance Group of Companies, American Isuzu Motors and Huffy Corporation.

Farmers provided substantial funding for the informational kiosks at the start of each byway which describes the area's natural cultural history and recreation opportunities. The kiosks will also include maps of the byways and reminders of the importance of appropriate outdoor behavior. Farmers magazine, *Friendly Exchange*, has also devoted feature articles to the Back Country Byways program.

American Isuzu Motors also provided major funding for the kiosks and has played an active role in the formal dedication of the national Back Country Byways program, near Mesquite, Nevada in the spring of 1990, and subsequent dedications of individual routes.

Huffy Corporation contributed bicycles to be used by BLM rangers patrolling the Back Country Byways and adjacent trails.

The partners in the BLM's program are dedicated to the protection of the designated Back Country Byways as well exposing more travelers to these truly scenic, historic, and cultural treasures.

LOCATIONS OF THE BACK COUNTRY BYWAYS

INTRODUCTION

Once, all the roads were trails—dusty, rutted ribbons that rolled across prairies, peaks, and plateaus. Beyond the trail, at the rainbow's end, lay a promised land, a new life, religious freedom, wealth. Today, that yearning to see what lies over the horizon, to find that illusive pot of gold at the road's end, is sustained by Americans.

A recent study indicates that forty-three percent of all Americans drive for pleasure. The National Scenic Byways program was created for these steering-wheel recreationists. First came the Scenic Byways, designated and maintained by the U.S. Forest Service on National Forest lands throughout the United States, in May, 1988. The Back Country Byways, a sister program administered by the Bureau of Land Management on its 272 million acres scattered across the West, was born in 1989.

BLM managers and recreation planners sat down, inventoried the scenic backroads in their districts, and selected thirty-eight roads that traversed 1,900 miles in eleven western states. Their picks showcase the beauty and diversity of America's public lands.

Other nominated roads now await approval and funding, further expanding the byway network.

The BLM plans eventually include information kiosks, like the one in the picture, along every Back Country Byway.

Wildlife abounds along the Back Country Byways. Here a mule deer grazes along Colorado's Alpine Loop Byway.

The Back Country Byways explore Oregon's lush Coast Range, thread over Colorado's lofty San Juan Mountains, follow Lewis and Clark's epic journey across Idaho and Montana, pass ancient Anasazi petroglyphs in Utah, and border the Rio Grande's wild gorge in New Mexico. Visitors find old forts, ghost towns, fossils, wildlife, hot springs, and stilled volcanos along the byways.

The BLM manages its lands, one-eighth of all the acreage in the United States, for multiple use. Each byway educates its travelers to those uses, including timber harvesting, cattle and sheep grazing, mining, and oil exploration.

The BLM, under director Cy Jamison, has also become increasingly aware that recreation is an important piece of the multiple use puzzle. The BLM now balances its traditional policy of multiple use and sustained yield with emerging programs emphasizing conservation, wildlife, wilderness, and recreation.

The Back Country Byways program demonstrates to visitors not only the many uses of public lands but their scenic diversity and recreational opportunities.

Outstanding recreation is found along the byways. Most of the lands are remote and unknown, providing solitude, wildness, and spectacular scenery. Few hiking trails are found on the byways, but there are plenty of places to hike. Just head cross-country though the sagebrush and junipers to the top of a nearby basalt-capped mesa. There are few established campgrounds, but there are plenty of places to camp. Find a spot that pleases you, set up the tent, build a fire, and watch the stars. Others hunt game—mule deer, elk, and pronghorn—on BLM land. There are plenty of places to fish, snowmobile, rock climb, observe wildlife, and look for fossils.

The BLM is designating all the byways with distinctive signs at their access points and at confusing intersections along the routes. Information kiosks and interpretative stations are being placed along the byways through funding by national corporations. The kiosks, which will be installed along Back Country Byways beginning in 1991 will feature a map of the byway and tips for travelers, as well as natural, historical and cultural interpretive material.

The Back Country Byways program is a way of discovering off-the-beaten track America. It's easy to take the Interstate or paved highway to get places, but the rarely trodden paths that wind across the mountains and canyons of the West beckon the adventurous traveler. He wants to take the road less traveled, to see new panoramas and scenic wonders, to revel in the rewards of the journey itself.

Back Country Byways—it's a phrase that conjures up images of dusty, rutted tracks; ranches nestled in tawny valleys; cloud shadows that trail across a dry lakebed; the sweet smell of sagebrush after a rain; and the song of a meadowlark atop a roadside fence. Out there, on the byways, a whole new world is waiting to be discovered. Its mountains, deserts, plains, rivers, and canyons are waiting for you.

Looking north from Oregon's Lakeview to Steens Byway.

DRIVING THE BYWAYS

It's easy to drive the Back Country Byways. Just pick one near your home or along your vacation route and head out. But keep in mind some basic rules and regulations before setting out and while driving along the byway. Be prepared for road emergencies and, above all, use common sense. It will get you through most bad situations.

Most of the byways are either paved or graded gravel and dirt roads, passable in ordinary passenger cars. But others are safely driven only in a high-clearance truck or four-wheel-drive vehicle. Some are closed in winter by heavy snows and after severe rain.

The BLM has divided the Back Country Byways into four types, depending on the road, its surface, and the vehicle needed to drive it. The four types are:

*Type I—These byways are either paved or have an all-weather surface. Normal passenger cars can easily negotiate the roads. They are usually narrow, slow-speed, secondary roads. None of the byways follow main highways.

*Type II—Roads that require high-clearance trucks or four-wheel-drive vehicles, although passenger cars may be able to negotiate them under good conditions. Check with the local BLM office for current road conditions. These roads are not paved but often have an improved gravel surface. They often cross dry, rocky arroyos, have rough, rutted sections, and have occasional steep grades and sharp curves.

*Type III—Byways requiring four-wheel-drive vehicles and others such as dirt bikes and all-terrain vehicles. These roads are often unimproved dirt tracks. Expect steep grades, rocky and muddy sections, and possible route-finding. Do not attempt these byways in a two-wheel-drive vehicle, the consequences could be serious for you and your car.

*Type IV—Trails that are managed for snowmobile, dirt bike, mountain bike, or ATV use.

Know your vehicle, its limits, and your driving ability. Use common sense before attempting a washed-out or dangerous road section. Help is a long way off on most of the byways. A ripped oil pan or accident can be disastrous. If you have any doubts, don't take chances. Turn around and try the road again another day. It will still be there—you might not be.

The byways are not high-speed roads. Drive slowly and don't invite disaster. Blind curves, steep grades, loose gravel surfaces, and narrow roads are encountered on almost all the byways. Although you probably won't encounter another traveler on most byways, always expect someone on sharp corners and blind hills. Keep to the right whenever possible and sound your horn if you can't see. Driving courtesy also gives uphill traffic the right-of-way. Look for turn-outs on narrow roads to allow them to pass. Always stop to lend aid or assistance. Keep to the designated roads. Driving across desert soils and

Many Back Country Byways pass through rugged, isolated territory. An ounce of preparation may prevent a pound of misery. La Madre Mountain and the Red Rock Canyon Byway in Nevada.

alpine tundra can damage them for hundreds of years.

Be prepared before setting out. Many byways cross dry, barren deserts where summer temperatures regularly climb over 100 degrees. Carry plenty of water. Five gallons is not too much.

Take extra food. Carry sleeping gear, spare clothing, rain gear, compass, maps, and first aid kit. A tool kit, shovel, set of tire chains, and extra fan belt should be stowed in the trunk. Be sure the spare tire is properly inflated. Make sure you carry enough gasoline to drive the byway.

If you do break down, sit in a juniper's shade, take a drink of water, and review your options. If it's late, the weather is bad, traffic is sparse, or you're in the desert, it's best to stay with your vehicle. It provides shelter. Otherwise you might walk out to a main road or ranch house—perhaps as far as twenty or thirty miles away—and flag down help. The universal distress call is a signal repeated three times—three shouts, three whistles, three horn blasts, three headlight flashes. Keep a calm head. As naturalist Ernest Thompson Seton wrote in 1906: "The worst thing you can do is get frightened...It robs the wanderer of his judgement and of his limb power; it is fear that turns the passing experience into a final tragedy...Keep cool and all will be well."

Weather along the byways can be unpredictable. In summer expect hot temperatures and heavy afternoon thunderstorms. Lightning is dangerous, particularly on high, isolated points. Rain can wash out road sections where byways cross or follow dry arroyos such as on the Bitter Springs Trail or turn

A National Back Country Byway sign marks the summit of Green Mountain on Oregon's Christmas Valley Byway.

the road into impassable gumbo as on the Missouri Breaks byway. Watch the weather and don't be afraid to turn back.

Camping is allowed on most BLM lands. Informal, undeveloped sites are popular with back country travelers. There is the freedom to camp where you want. There are no restrictions on pets. The sites are free. But there are also responsibilities.

Camping is limited to fourteen days at any one site. Campers need to pack out their trash, disperse the fire ring, and properly dispose of human waste. Campers must avoid camping within 100 feet of springs accessible to wildlife. Campfires should not be left unattended and throughly doused before leaving. Fires should be made of dead and down wood. Use a gas stove whenever possible. Try to camp at a previously used site, it minimizes impact on soil and vegetation. Pack out trash left by thoughtless visitors. It maintains scenic beauty and saves tax dollars. Respect other campers by keeping noise down and pets under control.

Many of the byways cross desert lands, and free-flowing water is rare. If you do find a stream of clear, cold water, remember to purify before you drink. Bacterial and protozoan contamination, particularly *Giardia*, can make you very sick. *Giardia*, spread by fecal contamination from infected humans and animals, thrives in cold streams and lakes. If you have to use stream water, boil it vigorously for ten minutes or screen it with a filter and use chemical purification. Also beware of water polluted by mining operations.

Respect mining claims, livestock fences, and private property. Report vandalism to the nearest BLM office. There are both state and federal laws protecting all antiquities on public lands, including prehistoric Indians ruins and artifacts, historic sites, fossilized wood and bone, and other items of scientific interest. Help preserve America's rich past by looking but not taking. Amateur collectors may keep certain fossils, gems, and petrified wood found on public lands. Check with the nearest BLM office to locate these rockhounding areas.

TAKE PRIDE IN AMERICA is a national campaign to encourage everyone who visits our public lands to take pride in them, to leave them better for those who follow, and to protect them for future Americans. Our historic and natural resources are irreplaceable. Treat them with the care and respect they deserve.

Use good outdoor manners and common sense when traveling our Back Country Byways. It's worth the effort.

MAP LEGEND

Byway	▬▬▬▬	Interstate	(00)
4-Wheel Only Byway	▭▬▭▬	U.S. Highway	(00)
Interstate and Four Lane Highways	⇒	State or Other Principal Road	(00)
All Other Roads (Paved)	⇒	Forest Road	[000]
Unpaved Roads	======	Pass	)(
Hiking Trail	············	Mountain Peak	+
Point of Interest	■	River, Creek	∿
Picnic Area	⊼	Wash	⌇
Campground	▲	Waterfall	//
Mine	⛏	Lakes	⬭
Cemetery	†	Map Scale	0 1 2 3 Miles

NATIONAL FOREST BOUNDARY

WILDERNESS BOUNDARY

STATE BOUNDARY

Arizona

N

HUALAPAI MOUNTAIN
Arizona

General description: A forty-five-mile Type I, II, and III byway, with paved, gravel, and four-wheel sections, that traverses the crest of the rugged Hualapai Mountains in west-central Arizona between Kingman and Yucca.

Special attractions: Hualapai Mountain Park, hiking, camping, picnicking, Wild Cow Springs Recreation Site, birdwatching, Wabayuma Wilderness Study Area, old mines, saguaro cacti.

Location: Hualapai Mountains in west-central Arizona between Kingman and Yucca, south of Interstate 40.

Byway route numbers and names: Hualapai Mountain Road, BLM Road #2123, Boriana Canyon Road.

Travel season: Spring, summer, and fall. In winter the four-wheel drive section of the drive can be slick and blocked by snow. The lower sections are accessible in winter.

Camping: Hualapai Mountain Park has campsites, group campsites, and rental cabins. Wild Cow Springs Campground, operated by the BLM, has campsites and restrooms, but no water.

Services: All services in Kingman. Limited services in Yucca.

Nearby attractions: Kingman, Havasu National Wildlife Refuge, Lake Havasu, Lake Mead National Recreation Area, Old Route 66-Oatman Road National Back Country Byway, Parker Dam Back Country Byway, Grand Canyon Caverns.

For more information: BLM, Kingman Resource Area Office, 2475 Beverly Avenue, Kingman AZ. (602) 757-3161.

The Trip: The byway travels through the Hualapai Mountains, the highest range in western Arizona. The road, climbing almost 5,000 feet above Kingman and the Sacramento Valley, passes through a wide variety of ecosystems. Traveling over the Hualapai Mountains is like taking a telescoped journey from Mexico to Montana—all in the space of a little more than ten miles, the distance from Kingman to Hualapai Mountain Park.

Along the byway's lower elevations, particularly on its southern end in Boriana Canyon, the road traverses a mixture of Sonoran and Mojave desert plants, including the northernmost stand of saguaro cacti. Atop the byway's mountain crest at 7,000 feet, it passes through wind-ruffled ponderosa pine forests, broken by groves of fir and quaking aspen.

The forty-five-mile-long byway has four distinct road segments. The first segment, Hualapai Mountain Road, is thirteen miles of paved two-lane road that climbs from the corner of Stockton Hill Road and Andy Devine Avenue in Kingman to Hualapai Mountain Park in the saddle between Hayden Peak and Dean Peak. The second section, from the park to Wild Cow Springs Recreation Site, is a six-mile, unpaved, mostly one-lane road. Both segments can be safely driven in passenger cars.

The twenty-one-mile third segment from Wild Cow Springs to Boriana Mine is rough and single lane. It requires a high-clearance, four-wheel-drive vehicle. The last part, from Boriana Mine to Yucca on Interstate 40, is twelve miles

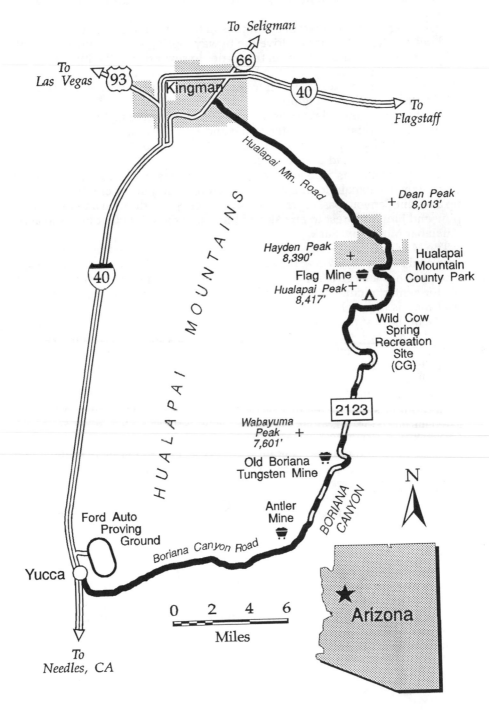

To Seligman

To Las Vegas — 93

66

40

Kingman

To Flagstaff

Hualapai Mtn. Road

Dean Peak 8,013'

HUALAPAI MOUNTAINS

Hayden Peak 8,390'

Flag Mine

Hualapai Peak 8,417'

Hualapai Mountain County Park

40

Wild Cow Spring Recreation Site (CG)

2123

Wabayuma Peak 7,601'

Old Boriana Tungsten Mine

BORIANA CANYON

N

Antler Mine

Ford Auto Proving Ground

Boriana Canyon Road

Yucca

Arizona

0 2 4 6
Miles

To Needles, CA

9

of dirt and gravel roadway suitable for passenger cars, although the five miles from Antler Mine to Boriana Mine are narrow and rocky. Visitors traversing the byway's entire length should plan on about six hours with stops.

Those without four-wheel drive can drive the Hualapai Mountain Road and the Boriana Canyon Road. Both are scenic and very different from each other.

Visitors can expect pleasant conditions in the Hualapais. Spring, summer, and fall are the best times to drive the byway. Spring and fall have pleasant warm days with temperatures in the forties to seventies in the higher elevations and fifties to nineties in the lower canyons. Summer temperatures in the lower elevations reach well into the 100s, while mountain temperatures are in the seventies or eighties.

Nights can be cool. Elevations above 6,000 feet receive eighteen to twenty inches of precipitation annually. Snow and rain close the four-wheel drive section of the byway in winter, although the Hualapai Mountain Road and Boriana Canyon Road are passable.

The byway begins in Kingman, just off Interstate 40, and heads south toward the Hualapai Mountains up a paved road. It quickly climbs ten miles up Sawmill Canyon, passing from Mojave desert scrub through a thick pinyon pine and juniper forest to an oak and pine forest at 6,500 feet in 2,320-acre Hualapai Mountain Park.

The Mojave County-owned park spreads across the forested saddle between Hualapai Peak, at 8,417-feet the range's high point, and 8,013-foot Dean Peak. The park has a large campground, rental cabins, water, restrooms, a small visitor center, picnic facilities, and an excellent fifteen-mile trail system. A trail map is available at the visitor center.

One of the best trails climbs 1.9 miles west from the campground up steep slopes to a lofty lookout atop 8,396-foot Hayden Peak. The summit view is spectacular—west over the Black Mountains to hazy ranges in California, north toward the high plateaus of the Grand Canyon, and eastward to the sprawling Aquarius Mountains.

Past the park the byway becomes a narrow, twisting, gravel road that dips in and out of steep ridges just below the range crest. The road passes the gated entrance to the famous Flag Mine, where gold and silver were extracted from 1874 to 1929. The Hualapai Mountains, composed of Precambrian gneiss, schist, and granite, contain many rocks and minerals including one of the purest mica deposits in the world. Brush coats the slopes with gambel oak, manzanita, juniper, mountain mahogany, and groves of ponderosa pine and walnut trees tucked in moist north-facing ravines. Wild Cow Springs Recreation Site, managed by the BLM, is reached after six miles. The primitive campground has campsites, restrooms, grills, tables, but no water. It's also the end of the road for passenger cars.

The byway's next twenty-one miles, requiring four-wheel-drive vehicles, traverses the lofty crest of the Hualapais. Every corner along the road yields great views and there are adaquate pull-offs to enjoy them. The BLM plans trailheads along the byway for paths into the proposed Wabayuma Peak Wilderness Area that borders the byway on the west. Wabayuma Peak, a sharply pointed 7,061-foot peak, was named for Wauba-Yuma, a Walapai Indian chief killed for revenge in 1866.

This remote stretch of road harbors a rich variety of wildlife. Mountain lion, mule deer, rabbits, coyotes, bobcats, raccoons, skunks, and squirrels

Ruins of the old Antler Mine scatter across Boriana Canyon on the Hualapai Mountains Byway.

live throughout the range. The Hualapais are also home to the only elk herd in western Arizona.

Antelope Wash below Wild Cow Spring is the historic habitat for the endangered Hualapai Mexican vole. Over eighty bird species have been identified in the Wild Cow Spring area, including hawks, owls, whippoorwills, hummingbirds, flycatchers, warblers, and Gambel quail. The range's fifteen reptiles include the Sonoran mountain kingsnake, blacktailed rattlesnake, western blackheaded rattlesnake, and Arizona black rattlesnake.

After the Wabayuma Peak trailhead, the byway plunges down from the range crest to the abandoned Boriana Mine, once one of Arizona's largest tungsten producers. Below the mine the road follows Boriana Canyon through an area of exceptional beauty. The steep-walled canyon, filled with sharp needle peaks and rounded granite crags, is rough, raw desert country. What is unusual here is the unique mixture of Sonoran and Mojave desert plant communities. Tall, stately saguaro cacti, symbol of the southern Sonoran Desert, grow side by side with gnarly Joshua trees, the dominant large plant of the Mojave Desert. In this western Arizona canyon, the two deserts meet and mingle.

The byway leaves Boriana Canyon on a two-lane gravel road and travels ten miles over a broad outwash plain below the Hualapai Mountains to the small town of Yucca, twenty-five miles south of Kingman on Interstate 40. Over 100 years ago Yucca was one of western Arizona's largest gold mining towns. The byway segment from Yucca to Boriana Mine can be driven in a passenger car.

2 WILD HORSE CANYON
California

General description: A twelve-mile, Type II dirt byway that makes a horseshoe-shaped loop connecting two BLM campgrounds in the unique East Mojave National Scenic Area.

Special attractions: Scenic views, volcanic formations, desert wildlife, camping, hiking, picnicking.

Location: Southeastern California in the East Mojave National Scenic Area between Interstates 15 and 40. The southern end of the byway is seventeen miles north of Interstate 40 from the Mitchell Caverns/Providence Mountains State Park exit. The northern end is thirty-five miles south of Interstate 15 via the Kelso-Cima Road.

Byway route name: BLM Wild Horse Canyon Road.

Travel season: Year-round. Best times, of course, are in the fall, winter, and spring when temperatures are moderate. Summers are hot, with temperatures in the surrounding lowlands regularly reaching 110 degrees and above. Temperatures along the byway, which ranges from 4,200 feet to 5,600 feet in elevation, are usually up to twenty degrees cooler than on the desert floor. Severe thunderstorms in summer can cause flash flooding and make the byway route impassable.

Camping: Two BLM campgrounds are at either end of the byway. Hole-in-the-Wall, at the south end, has twenty-three campsites in a picturesque setting among volcanic cliffs. Mid Hills Campground, near the byway's north terminus, has twenty-six shady sites. Both areas have tables, grills, fire pits, water, and pit toilets. Hole-in-the-Wall has an RV dump station. A daily fee of $4.00 per unit is charged. Primitive camping is allowed along the byway, and in existing campsites.

Services: No services along the byway. Limited services are available in Goffs.

Nearby attractions: Mitchell Caverns in Providence Mountains State Recreation Area, Kelso Dunes, Devil's Playground, Cinder Cones, Cima Dome, New York Mountains, Lake Mead National Recreation Area.

For more information: BLM, California Desert District Office, 1695 Spruce Street, Riverside, CA 92507. (714) 276-6394. BLM, Needles Resource Area Office, 101 W. Spikes Road, Needles, CA 92363. (619) 326-3896.

The Trip: Wild Horse Canyon Back Country Byway, the first byway dedicated in the BLM's Back Country Byway System in June of 1989, makes an open, horseshoe-shaped loop through the Mid-Hills in the heart of the East Mojave National Scenic Area.

The 1.5-million acre scenic area is a place of stark beauty with twenty-six rugged mountain ranges, the huge Kelso Dune field, Joshua tree forests, cave systems, wide basins, sharp volcanic features, and a human history that dates back more than 10,000 years.

The byway threads through Wild Horse Canyon along a wash that drains the Mid Hills, a low section of rolling granite and volcanic hills between the higher Providence Mountains to the south and the spectacular New York Mountains to the north. The byway, a dirt track with some sandy sections along the wash, can be driven by two-wheel drive vehicles with high-clearance. Summer thunderstorms sometimes render the road impassable. Watch for signs at the beginning of the byway warning of road closure. Adequate pulloffs for both passing and views are regularly found along the road. The byway takes a leisurely one to two hours to drive.

Weather in the Wild Horse Canyon area can be unpredictable. Fall, winter, and spring offer perhaps the best weather for travel, although temperature fluctuations, particularly in winter, can be very wide. Spring and fall

Wild Horse Canyon Byway follows a broad desert valley north of Wild Horse Mesa in the East Mojave National Scenic Area.

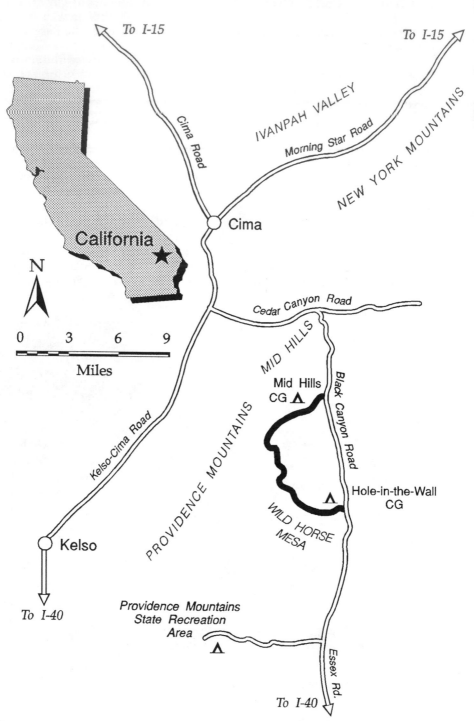

To I-15

To I-15

Cima Road

IVANPAH VALLEY

Morning Star Road

NEW YORK MOUNTAINS

California

N

0   3   6   9

Miles

Cima

Cedar Canyon Road

MID HILLS

Mid Hills CG

Black Canyon Road

PROVIDENCE MOUNTAINS

Kelso-Cima Road

Hole-in-the-Wall CG

WILD HORSE MESA

Kelso

To I-40

Providence Mountains State Recreation Area

Essex Rd.

To I-40

temperatures are generally between sixty and ninety degrees, with many clear or partly cloudy days. Springtime often brings windy periods. Winters can be cold and damp, with both rain and snow showers in the mountain ranges. Daytime highs range from forty to seventy degrees. Expect summer temperatures in the desert basins to exceed 110 degrees daily. In the mountains, including the Mid-Hills, temperatures are more moderate, usually in the 80 to 100 range. Nights can be cool in summer.

Wild Horse Canyon Byway begins a quarter-mile south of Hole-in-the-Wall Campground off Black Canyon Road, seventeen miles north of Interstate 40. The twenty-three-site campground is set against ragged volcanic cliffs. This area is great for exploring. Its weirdly eroded rock cliffs are full of holes, cavities, and arches. An unmaintained trail begins at the west end of the campground and twists through the cliffs. You descend metal rings in the rock at one place, before emerging into an open box canyon with scenic views west to Wild Horse Mesa. An eight-mile-long maintained trail connects Hole-in-the-Wall Campground with Mid Hills Campground.

The byway follows Wild Horse Canyon as it heads westward below long, flat Wild Horse Mesa. The mesa is capped by dark basalt cliffs formed by vast lava flows that once spread across the lower Mid Hills. Cholla cacti and Mojave yucca border the road. Just after the road begins, a rough seven-mile trail heads north to the Mid Hills Campground. After a couple miles, the byway turns north up a gravel and sand-filled wash and passes through rock portals. Stop and hike into the hills here. Cacti stud the hillsides and spring wildflowers add color to the drab landscape.

The Mid Hills, because of their elevation and variety of plant communities, is a good place to see wildlife. Rare desert bighorn sheep hide in the rugged mountains, along with mountain lion and bobcat. Mule deer browse in the wash along the road in early evening. Other animals seen are coyotes, kit foxes, antelope ground squirrels, packrats, rattlesnakes, lizard, and the protected desert tortoise. If you see a tortoise in the road, drive slowly around it. Don't pick it up and take it home. The tortoise is an endangered species, and if it is to survive we need to let them be. The rugged cliffs and mountains provide ideal habitat for birds of prey. Alert birdwatchers can sight golden eagles, prairie falcons, and a variety of hawks and owls.

The byway starts climbing past the rock portals, and with the ascent both temperatures and plants dramatically change from the lower elevations. Slowly the road leaves the sharp, angular volcanic landscape of the lower valley, and enters a region of old, rounded hills broken by outcrops of brilliant white granite. At the top of the byway spreads a thick pinyon pine and juniper forest with open areas filled with sagebrush. This plant community is typical of the Great Basin Desert several hundred miles to the north. The Mojave Desert lies between two of North America's most unique deserts—the hot, dry Sonoran Desert to the south, and the Great Basin Desert, a cold, high desert to the north.

The upper road gives breathtaking views of the surrounding desert. The needle peaks of the Providence Mountains, including 7,171-foot Providence Peak, prick the southern horizon, and west lie serrated desert ranges and sand dunes shimmering in the bright sunlight. Also on the upper byway is Mid Hills Campground.

This twenty-six-site campground, with shady tables and cool nights, is popular from spring through fall. The campground area, at 5,600 feet, offers fine hiking, scenic views, rock climbing, wildlife watching, and lots of desert quiet. Two more miles of byway road brings you back to Black Canyon Road. An eight-mile drive south takes you to Hole-in-the Wall.

A must-see attraction for any byway visitor is Providence Mountains State Recreation Area and its centerpiece, Mitchell Caverns, south of Hole-in-the-Wall and seventeen miles north of Interstate 40 on Essex Road. The Visitor Center, six-site campground, and caverns are perched at 4,300 feet on the steep eastern flank of Providence Peak. The limestone cavern, El Pakiva and Tecopa caves, can be visited on a guided tour at 1:30 p.m. on weekdays and 10 a.m., 1:30 and 3 p.m. on weekends from September 16 through June 15. The caves, developed by silver prospector Jack Mitchell, were used by the Chemehuevi Indians for hundreds of years. Remains of a 15,000-year-old Pleistocene ground sloth have been found in the cave.

3 BARREL SPRINGS
California

General description: A Type II, 20-mile, single-lane, gravel road over a high plateau in northeastern California and northwestern Nevada.

Special attractions: Scenic views, wildlife, solitude, hiking, primitive camping.

Location: In Modoc County, California and Washoe County, Nevada. Western access is from Fort Bidwell, California via Modoc County Road 6. Eastern access is from Cedarville via California Highway 299, Nevada Highway 34, Nevada Highway 8A, and the Mosquito Valley Road.

Byway route name: Marrel Springs Road.

Travel season: May through mid-November. Heavy snow and mud closes the road during winter and spring months. Mosquito Valley Road, the eastern access, is impassable in summer after heavy rains.

Camping: Primitive camping is allowed along the byway. An established primitive campground is at Fee Reservoir south of the byway's western access.

Services: Limited services are available at Fort Bidwell and Cedarville. Travelers should be self-contained, with sufficient gasoline, water, supplies, and equipment when driving the byway.

Nearby attractions: Buckhorn Back Country Byway, South Warner Wilderness Area, Modoc National Forest, Goose Lake, Modoc National Wildlife Refuge, Lakeview to Steens Back Country Byway.

For more information: BLM, Susanville District Office, 705 Hall Street, Susanville, CA 96130. (916) 257-5381.

The Trip: The Barrel Springs Back Country Byway crosses a high, upland plateau from Surprise Valley in northeastern California to Mosquito Valley in northwestern Nevada. Scenic views of the surrounding valleys and lofty peaks in the Warner Mountains to the west are splendid.

The byway is gravel, single-lane, and has numerous turnouts along its winding course. An open loop drive from Fort Bidwell, over the byway, down Mosquito Valley, and west to Cedarville takes two to three hours and is about

Barrel Springs Byway crosses Mosquito Valley and climbs a mesa's steep eastern escarpment.

sixty miles long. Elevations range from about 4,600 feet at its start near Fort Bidwell to almost 7,000 feet at its crest above Mosquito Valley.

The byway is open for traffic from mid-May to mid-November. It closes during winter and spring due to heavy snowfall and thick mud. Summer thunderstorms often make the eastern access road through Mosquito Valley impassable with sticky mud. Don't attempt this road section if the weather is at all threatening or the road appears muddy. It's a long walk to the nearest ranch house and even further, up to fifty miles, to Cedarville and Fort Bidwell. Bear in mind when driving the byway that another vehicle might not pass on the road for one or two days.

Summer and fall visitors can expect pleasantly warm days, with temperatures between seventy and ninety-five degrees on the byway. Nights

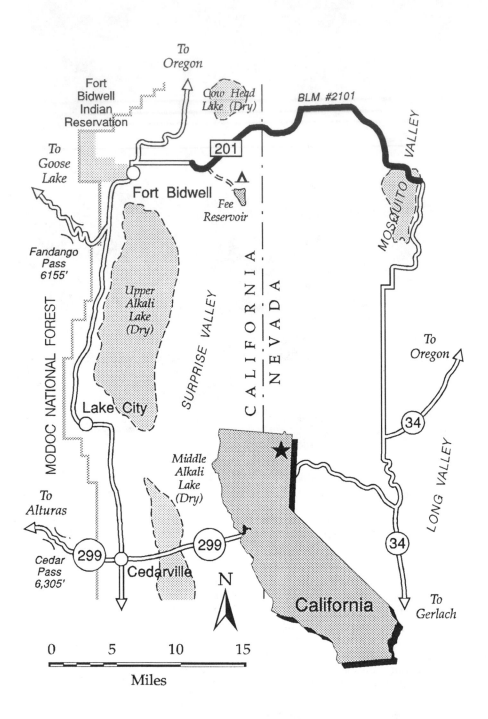

To Oregon

Fort Bidwell Indian Reservation

Cow Head Lake (Dry)

BLM #2101

MOSQUITO VALLEY

To Goose Lake

201

Fort Bidwell

Fee Reservoir

Fandango Pass 6155'

Upper Alkali Lake (Dry)

SURPRISE VALLEY

CALIFORNIA

NEVADA

To Oregon

34

MODOC NATIONAL FOREST

Lake City

Middle Alkali Lake (Dry)

LONG VALLEY

To Alturas

299

299

Cedarville

Cedar Pass 6,305'

N

California

34

To Gerlach

0   5   10   15
Miles

can be cool at the upper elevations. The byway lies in the rainshadow of the Warner Mountain escarpment to the west, so showers are usually brief and infrequent.

Begin the byway five miles east of Fort Bidwell via Modoc County Road 6 after crossing pastoral Surprise Valley. The road climbs up the sagebrush-covered flank of a huge swelling plateau, its rolling surface broken by abrupt, shallow, boulder-choked canyons that slice into hard, volcanic bedrock.

Atop the plateau, the byway wends eastward, passing range cattle and scrubby juniper trees. Broad, intermittent lakes shelter behind upheaved ridges, providing habitat for waterfowl in early summer. Other animals commonly seen along the road include mule deer, pronghorn antelope, hawks, eagles, and vultures. After thirteen miles the road bends south under the brow of a 7,099-foot mesa. Groves of quaking aspens add green and, in autumn, gold, to the grey sagebrush tapestry spread over the land.

The byway reaches its high point in a rocky saddle between two mesas rimmed by ancient lava flows. Stop at a pulloff where dramatic views unfold to the east. Below lies the white glare of dry Mosquito Lake, the byway road as it switchbacks down the steep hillside, and small springs that form shiny ponds surrounded by tall grass and reflecting the sky blue. Eastward lie unnamed and uninhabited mountains, their barren slopes lifted up over dry lakebeds, and abandoned ranches and homesteads left by their owners to spiders, ravens, and the rush of wind. Out here on this viewpoint you'll find the byway's essence—the freedom of distant horizons and the solitude of untrampled space.

Dropping quickly down into Mosquito Valley, the byway crosses Mosquito Lake on an elevated roadbed to its official end. Head south on the Mosquito Valley Road and into the western edge of Long Valley. After about twenty miles the road connects with Nevada Highways 34 and 8A, then California Highway 299 which goes west to Cedarville. The Barrel Springs Byway can easily be combined with the Buckhorn Byway to the south as a full day's exploration. Primitive camping is allowed along the byway and at Fee Reservoir south of the byway's western access near Fort Bidwell.

4 EAST MOJAVE SCENIC AREA
California

General description: The eight byways cross 222 miles of the spectacular East Mojave National Scenic Area in southeastern California.

Special attractions: Camping, picnicking, hiking, scenic views, desert plants and wildlife, spring wildflower displays, Cima Dome, Providence Mountains, Hole-in-the-Wall, Mitchell Caverns, New York Mountains, Kelso Dunes.

Location: Southeastern California in the East Mojave National Scenic Area between Interstates 15 and 40.

Travel season: Year-round. Summers are hot, with valley temperatures often exceeding 110 degrees. Temperatures in the mountain highlands are generally ten to twenty degrees cooler. Winter is cool and damp, with daily highs

Joshua trees line the byways in the East Mojave Scenic Area.

between forty and seventy degrees. Spring and fall are pleasant times to visit the area, with warm days and cool nights.

Camping: Primitive camping is allowed anywhere on public lands within the East Mojave National Scenic Area. The BLM has established campgrounds with water and tables at Mid Hills Campground on the Wild Horse Canyon Byway and Hole-in-the-Wall Campground on the Black Canyon Byway. Another campground is at Mitchell Caverns in the Providence Mountains State Recreation Area at the end of the Essex Road Byway.

Services: Limited services are found in the East Mojave Scenic Area. Baker on Interstate 15 has all services.

Nearby attractions: Lake Mead National Recreation Area, Joshua Tree National Monument, Amboy Crater, Death Valley National Monument, Lake Havasu, Las Vegas.

For more information: BLM, California Desert Information Center, 831 Barstow Road, Barstow, CA 92311, (619) 256-8617. BLM, Needles Resource Area, P.O. Box 888, Needles, CA 92363, (619) 326-3896.

The Trip: Eight Back Country Byways—Kelbaker Road, Kelso-Cima Road, Cima Road, Black Canyon Road, Ivanpah-Lanfair Road, Essex Road, Cedar Canyon Road, and Wildhorse Canyon Road—form a 222-mile-long network across the immense East Mojave National Scenic Area. The area's 1.5 million acres of mountains, plains, valleys, gorges, and sand dunes are administered by the Bureau of Land Management. The area's byway system criss-crosses the sprawling region, offering visitors the opportunity to view a desert of magnificent diversity and beauty.

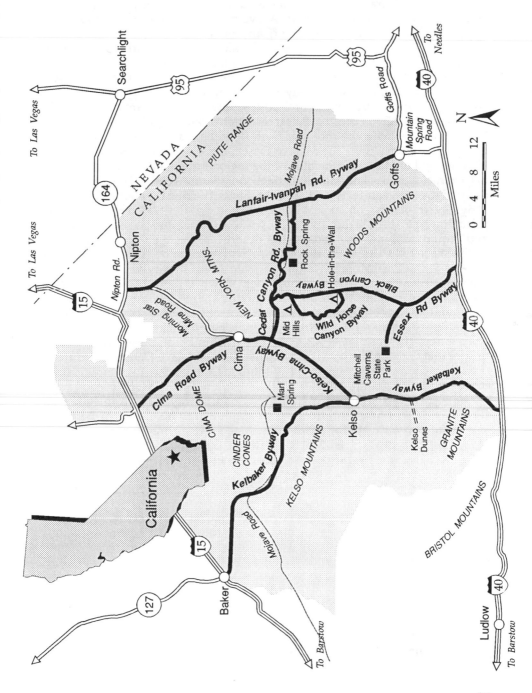

The byways are two-lane and accessible in a normal passenger car. Most are paved, although the Black Canyon, Cedar Canyon, Wildhorse Canyon, and Ivanpah-Lanfair roads are mostly unpaved. The different byways can be combined into loop drives. Traffic is generally light, although weekends can be busy.

Be prepared when driving the byways, particularly during the hot summer months. Make sure your vehicle's gas tank and spare tire are full before setting out. Carry plenty of water. A five-gallon container is not too much for a day trip. If you're heading off any of the byways, take extra food, clothing, and a sleeping bag. If you do break down, stay with your vehicle. Be alert for extreme road damage after summer flashfloods.

Spring and fall are the best times for traveling the East Mojave byways. Daily high temperatures generally range from sixty to ninety degrees, with cool nights. Spring afternoons are often windy. Summers are hot. Highs in the low valleys often exceed 110 degrees. Nights can be cold. Violent summer thunderstorms, with the threat of flash flooding, rumble across the desert on summer afternoons. The Mojave Desert has two distinct wet seasons in summer and winter, with the bulk of the region's annual precipitation falling between November and March. Expect cool, damp weather in winter, with daily highs between forty and seventy. Snow flurries fly above 3,000 feet.

Byway travelers can expect to see a wide variety of desert wildlife, including mule deer, bighorn sheep, coyotes, kit foxes, and occasional bobcats and mountain lions. The endangered desert tortoise is also seen. A loss of desirable habitat threatens the tortoise with extinction. One of their last refuges is the East Mojave National Scenic Area. Byway visitors can help the tortoise survive by driving around them slowly if they are plodding across the road, not picking them up, and leaving them at home in the desert. Removing a tortoise from the wild is not only illegal, but removes its reproductive potential. Unlawful collection has decimated tortoise populations across the Southwest. Careful stewardship by all desert visitors will ensure that this rare reptile will remain part of the Mojave Desert community.

Each of the byways, except the Wildhorse Canyon Byway which is fully discussed in a separate chapter, will be explored from west to east.

The Type I, sixty-mile-long Kelbaker Road Byway runs from Baker on Interstate 15 southeast to Interstate 40 about eighty miles east of Barstow. The road, paved except for a five-mile graded dirt section, traverses a spectacular section of the East Mojave National Scenic Area.

East of Baker, the byway passes Cinder Cones National Natural Landmark. This collection of thirty-two volcanic cinder cones erupted between 800 and 1,000 years ago. Past the cones, the road bends south and reaches Kelso 35 miles from Baker. Kelso, named for a railroad official, was established in 1905 as a water stop on the San Pedro, Los Angeles, and Salt Lake Railroad. Gold and silver discoveries in the Providence Mountains and iron ore mines made Kelso a boomtown, with a population of 2,000 in the 1940s.

Kelso Dunes, at 600 feet the third highest dune field in the United States, lies west of the byway. These dramatic white dunes gleam in the desert's brilliant sunlight. Westerly winds that regularly scour the Mojave River floodplain and the Devil's Playground have slowly built the towering dunes over the last 100,000 years. The dune field covers forty-five square miles. Spring brings a flood of wildflowers to the dunes, including desert primrose, sand verbana, and sunflowers. Animals living here include the kangaroo

A visitor along the Cima Road Byway in the East Mojave Scenic Area.

rat and the sidewinder rattlesnake. A hike to the dune high point takes about two hours.

South of the Kelso Dunes turnoff, the byway becomes gravel for five miles. The ragged Granite Mountains loom west of the road. The byway ends at the Kelbaker Exit on Interstate 40, eighty miles east of Barstow.

The Type I Cima Road Back County Byway stretches seventeen miles from the Cima Road Exit on Interstate 15 south to Cima. The paved road heads south from the Interstate past Cima Dome. The dome, a quartz monzonite (a rock similar to granite) batholith about seventy-five square miles in size, lifts its rounded form over 1,500 feet above the surrounding desert playas. The dome is well known for its fine and extensive Joshua tree forests. Eleven miles south of

Interstate 15 lies Sunrise Rocks, a good place to stop and explore or picnic and camp. A two-mile trail to 5,755-foot Teutonia Peak, a small, craggy peak on Cima Dome, begins north of Sunrise Rock. The byway offers marvelous views of the Providence Mountains and Kelso Dunes to the south and the Ivanpah Mountains to the east. The byway ends at Cima, a mostly abandoned town that once served as a railroad siding and ranching and mining center.

The Kelso-Cima Byway, a twenty-mile-long, paved, Type I byway, travels from Cima to Kelso alongside the railroad tracks. Both towns were originally railroad stops on the old San Pedro, Los Angeles, and Salt Lake Railroad. They also have served as centers for mining and ranching activity in the Mojave Desert. The road, following a broad, open valley studded with Joshua trees and creosote bushes, offers striking views of the rugged Providence Mountains to the east, the shining Kelso Dunes to the southwest, and the rounded hump of Cima Dome to the north. At Kelso the byway hooks up with Kelbaker Road Byway.

The Cedar Canyon Road Back Country Byway, a Type I, twenty-five-mile-long, graded dirt byway, is the major route connecting the east and west parts of the East Mojave National Scenic Area. The byway roughly follows the historic Mojave Road, a former Indian trail that connected coastal villages with the Colorado River. By the mid-eighteenth century, the U.S. Army made the trail into a wagon road from Los Angeles to Prescott, Arizona. Army supply trains, immigrant wagons, stagecoaches, and mail regularly traveled over the road. Railroads, in the 1880s, rendered the Mojave Road obsolete. In 1983 the 138-mile-long road, through the efforts of the Friends of the Mojave Road, reopened as an historical and recreational road. Most of the road is four-wheel-drive only.

The Cedar Canyon byway begins about four and a half miles south of Cima on the Kelso-Cima byway. Turn east, bump over the railroad tracks, and begin climbing a long, sloping bajada toward the Mid Hills. After four miles the paved road turns to graded dirt. The junction with the Black Canyon byway is reached at six miles. Further east lies Rock Springs, an important desert watering hole on the Mojave Road. Camp Rock Spring, a lonely U.S. Army outpost to protect travelers and mail, was established here in December, 1866. The trickling spring is surrounded by rock walls decorated with Indian petroglyphs and Army graffiti. The byway ends on the Lanfair-Ivanpah Road Back Country Byway fifteen miles north of Goffs.

The Black Canyon byway, a twenty-mile, Type I, graded dirt road, runs south from Cedar Canyon Road byway to Essex Road byway through the Mid Hills and past high volcanic mesas. The road climbs up from Cedar Canyon through a pinyon pine and juniper woodland, across rolling sagebrush flats, and then down through a sharp, dry canyon to Hole-in-the-Wall. Here, a twenty-three-site BLM campground is set among bizarrely eroded volcanic cliffs. The BLM also manages a Visitor Center here that offers information on the East Mojave National Scenic Area. The Type II Wildhorse Canyon byway begins just south of the campground. There is excellent hiking and bird watching in the area. Springtime also brings spectacular wildflower displays to the desert floor. Continuing south, the byway rolls across a wide plain flanked by high mesas capped by basaltic lava flows and after nine miles ends on the Essex Road byway.

The Essex Road Back Country Byway begins on Interstate 40 at the Essex Road Exit 100 miles east of Barstow. The Type I, sixteen-mile, paved byway heads northwest from the Interstate across a wide, creosote-covered desert valley toward the towering Providence Mountains. After ten miles, the byway reaches an intersection with the Black Canyon Road byway. Continue straight ahead. After a couple more miles, the road climbs steeply up to its end at the 4,300-foot visitor center at Mitchell Caverns and the Providence Mountains State Recreation Area, a small state-owned preserve inside the East Mojave National Scenic Area.

The Providence Mountains, a ragged range of sharp limestone rock, has several caverns, including El Pakiva and Tecopa caves at Mitchell Caverns. They are well worth visiting. Guided mile-and-a-half tours are given daily in spring, summer, and fall. The small visitor center has informative displays on the area's history and natural history. There is also a short nature trail and a small 6-site campground that offers marvelous views east across the wide valley below to distant, hazy mountain ranges along the Colorado River. Providence Peak, the range high point at 7,171 feet, can be climbed directly from the campground up its steep rocky ridges. Wear stout boots and clothes, there are plenty of cacti among the rocks.

The Type I Lanfair-Ivanpah Road Back Country Byway is a fifty-five-mile-long paved and gravel road on the eastern edge of the East Mojave National Scenic Area. The middle twenty-five miles of the byway is gravel. The road's northern access is on Nipton road, three miles east of the Interstate 15 Nipton Road Exit. The byway heads south across the broad Ivanpah Valley, then over the rugged New York Mountains. This predominantly granite range reaches heights of 7,500 feet. High atop the mountains, where temperatures are cool and more rain falls than in the surrounding desert, are forests of white fir. Other woodlands of pinyon pine, juniper, and oak provide excellent wildlife habitat for bighorn sheep and mule deer.

Castle Buttes, a jagged outcrop of andesite spires and buttes north of the byway, provides spectacular scenery for byway travelers. A four-wheel-drive road allows access to the buttes for hiking and camping adventures. Another fine spot for exploring and camping is Caruthers Canyon in the New York Mountains. A relic stand of coastal chaparrel, left from wetter post-glacial times, grows in the canyon along with oak, manzanita, and Joshua trees.

Continuing south, the byway passes its junction with the Cedar Canyon byway, and heads across Lanfair Valley. The valley, named for early homesteader E.L. Lanfair, was farmed with corn and beans in the early twentieth century. East of the byway, on the eastern side of Lanfair Valley, lies scenic Piute Gorge, free-flowing Piute Creek, and historic Fort Piute, a Mojave Road army outpost. The byway ends at Goffs, an important railroad siding on the Atlantic and Pacific Railroad in the 1880s. Helper engines based here pulled trains up the long uphill grade from Needles on the Colorado River. From Goffs, the road continues south to Interstate 40.

BUCKHORN
California

General description: A Type II, twenty-eight-mile, single-lane, gravel road through a typical Great Basin desert landscape in northeastern California and northwestern Nevada.

Special attractions: Wildlife watching, wild horses, hiking, primitive camping, solitude, extensive views.

Location: In Lassen County, California and Washoe County, Nevada, about sixty-five miles northeast of Susanville, California. The byway's western access is via U.S. Highway 395, Lassen County 502, and Lassen County Marr Road. Eastern access is from Nevada Highway 447 about thirty miles southeast of Eagleville, California.

Byway route name and number: Lassen County Road 526—Marr Road.

Travel season: Mid-May through mid-November. Snow and mud closes the road in winter and spring.

Camping: Primitive camping is allowed along the byway.

Services: Limited services are available at Eagleville, Litchfield, and Termo, California or Gerlach, Nevada. All are more than forty miles away from the byway.

Nearby attractions: Barrel Springs Back Country Byway, South Warner Wilderness Area, Lassen Volcanic National Park.

For more information: BLM, Susanville District Office, 705 Hall Street, Susanville, CA 96130. (916) 257-5381.

The Trip: The byway crosses twenty-eight miles of terrain representative of the upper Great Basin desert in far northeastern California and remote northwestern Nevada. It is a land of long views, distant mountain ranges, open sky, and solitude. The road is single-lane, gravel, lightly maintained, and has plenty of pull-offs for scenic views. It can be driven in a passenger car, although a high-clearance vehicle might be needed in places, depending on road conditions. The byway is easily driven in two hours.

Travelers can expect summer temperatures between eighty and ninety-five degrees. Fall temperatures are ten to thirty degrees cooler. Most of the byway is about 6,000 feet in elevation, but at its eastern end it drops to 4,700 feet at Duck Flat.

The drive begins on U.S. Highway 395, midway between Susanville and Alturas, California at Ravendale. Turn east on Lassen County 502, a roughly paved road that crosses a flat plain below the broad cones of Spanish Springs Peak and 7,964-foot Observation Peak. After about twelve miles keep right on gravel Lassen County 536, Marr Road, and go straight east toward the gentle hills ahead.

Buckhorn Byway officially begins at the base of the hills. The road bumps over a cattle guard and climbs from the plain up a sagebrush-covered hillside spotted with shapely western juniper trees. The byway goes past an area of sand dunes, stabilized with brush and trees, formed by persistent westerly winds scouring the wide basin west of the hills. Looking south down a canyon gives a view of mostly dry Buckhorn Lake, its alkali flats glistening in the sunlight.

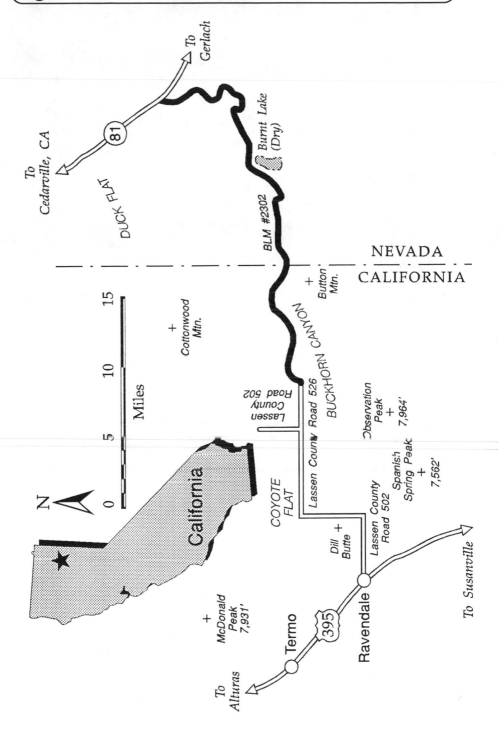

The Buckhorn Back Country Byway traverses spacious valleys below basalt-rimmed mesas in eastern California.

For the next twenty miles, the byway dips and rolls over the undulating hills, crossing shallow valleys and passing intermittent lakes. Occasional glimpses to the north reveal snowcapped peaks in the South Warner Wilderness Area.

The byway region, on the border of the Sierra Nevada and the Great Basin Desert, is a high, cold desert dominated by a single plant species—sagebrush or *Artemisia tridentata*. Below the rim of the hilltops, capped by ancient lava flows, grow scattered stands of quaking aspen and mountain mahogany, a favorite deer food. Western junipers also grow on the hillsides.

The country along the byway is remote and unpeopled. Travelers need to be prepared and carry emergency provisions, water, and equipment. In the event of a breakdown, it might be days before another vehicle passes. This wild character provides ideal habitat for animals that typically live in sagebrush areas, including pronghorn antelope, mule deer, coyote, badger, and soaring golden eagles and turkey vultures. Wild horses also roam these upland hills. The shallow intermittent lakes along the byway are home in early summer for waterfowl—ducks, geese, avocets, and killdeer.

Past Burnt Lake, a long, dry lakebed full of cattle grazing on short grass, the byway climbs past swells of lichen-encrusted black lava cliffs to a lofty viewpoint into Nevada. To the east, ragged mountain ridges in the Granite Range etch their outlines against the sky, while below lies the sere playa of Duck Flat. The byway drops steeply from here, leaving the sagebrush and juniper behind as it winds down into the dry valley of saltbush and shadscale.

Near road's end sits an abandoned, sunbaked ranch, its wooden corrals and buildings crumbling, its windmill idle. The byway ends on the edge of Duck Flat on Nevada Highway 447. Gerlach, Nevada lies about forty miles southeast, while Eagleville, California sits thirty miles northwest.

6   ALPINE LOOP
Colorado

General description: A sixty-three-mile, Type III byway that traverses the rugged and scenic San Juan Mountains between Ouray, Silverton, and Lake City.

Special attractions: Lake City National Historic District, Capitol City, Rose's Cabin, Engineer Pass, Big Blue Wilderness Area, Animas Forks, Silverton National Historic District, Ouray National Historic District, Cinnamon Pass, American Basin, five 14,000-foot peaks, Lake San Cristobal, Weminuche Wilderness Area, hiking, climbing, fishing, four-wheeling, scenic views, camping, picnicking, old mines, backpacking, mountain biking, wildlife, wildflowers.

Location: The San Juan Mountains in southwestern Colorado. The byway's western accesses are from U.S. 550 just south of Ouray and from Silverton up Colorado Highway 110. The eastern access is on Colorado Highway 149 at Lake City, sixty-five miles southwest of Gunnison.

Byway route names and numbers: Colorado Highways 110 and 149, Engineer Pass Road, Cinnamon Pass Road, Mineral Creek Road.

Travel season: The entire byway is open from July into October. Heavy snow closes the high roads the rest of the year. The lower roads open earlier in the season. Check with the BLM office for road conditions.

Camping: Primitive camping is allowed along the byway, except for the road section between Lake City and Capitol City. A fourteen day camping limit is imposed. Established campgrounds on the byway are Mill Creek (22 sites) and Williams Creek (21 sites) campgrounds. Ampitheater Campground, off U.S. 550 just south of Ouray, has thirty-three campsites. Private campgrounds in Ouray, Silverton, and Lake City provide full services.

Services: All services in Ouray, Silverton, and Lake City.

Nearby attractions: Telluride, Yankee Boy Basin, Imogene Pass, Ophir Pass, Lizard Head Wilderness Area, Mt. Sneffels Wilderness Area, San Juan Scenic Skyway, Rio Grande National Forest, Uncompahgre National Forest, Curecanti National Recreation Area, Black Canyon of the Gunnison National Monument, Powderhorn Primitive Area, Durango and Silverton Narrow Gauge Railroad, Durango, Mesa Verde National Park.

For more information: BLM, Montrose District, 2465 S. Townsend, Montrose, CO 81401. (303) 249-7791.

The Trip: The Alpine Loop Back Country Byway threads through the scenic San Juan Mountains. It climbs over two lofty passes, traverses steep-walled river valleys, passes alpine meadows sprinkled with wildflowers, stops at historic ghost towns and mines, and offers a wealth of outdoor recreation.

Silverton, a National Historic District, lies at the southern end of the Alpine Loop Byway.

The byway, linking Lake City, Silverton, and Ouray, follows roads first built by miners over 100 years ago for hauling freight and ore.

Much of the Type III byway is accessible by passenger cars and high-clearance vehicles, but the high passes can be crossed only by four-wheel-drive. The Engineer and Cinammon Pass roads are extremely rough, steep, and narrow. Know your vehicle's limits, and don't stray beyond them. Frequent heavy rain and even summer snow makes the roads slippery. Uphill traffic always has the right-of-way. Keep track of turnouts along narrow roads to allow others to safely pass. All vehicles are limited to designated roads, marked by white arrows, to lessen the environmental impact. Traffic is generally moderate, although weekends can be busy. Allow a full day to drive the entire byway.

Expect variable, unpredictable weather. Summer and fall days are generally cool, ranging from forty to seventy-five degrees. Nights can be cold, even in August, and often dip below freezing. Severe thunderstorms drop torrents of rain, sleet, and snow regularly on summer afternoons. Lightning on the high passes is very dangerous. Be prepared for every possible weather condition.

Carry extra layers of clothing and rain gear. It is easy to get sunburned in the thin air. Use sunglasses and sunscreen to protect yourself.

The byway is a loop with three access points—Lake City, Silverton, and Ouray. Lake City is a popular starting point. The town, now a National Historic District, got its start in 1874 as an outfitting and distribution center for nearby mines. The Golden Fleece, one of the richest, turned it into a boomtown. Alfred Packer made the town famous after his conviction for the cannibalistic murders of five companions. Today, Lake City is the quiet county seat of Hinsdale County, one of the least populated counties in the United States.

The two-lane, gravel byway heads west from Lake City up Henson Creek. The Engineer Pass summit lies eighteen miles from Lake City. Steep cliffs line the road as it climbs. The road passes through Henson, the site of the Ute-Ulay Mine which opened in 1871. Below the byway spreads the ruins of a 118-foot-high dam that once provided power for a tramway and mill. The entire area is private property. Do not trespass.

The rough Nellie Creek Road, providing access to the Big Blue Wilderness Area and 14,309-foot Uncompahgre Peak, is reached after 5.5 miles. A couple miles past Nellie Creek, the canyon opens into a U-shaped valley carved by ancient glaciers.

Capitol City, at the junction of Henson and Matterhorn creeks, was the dream town of local mill owner George T. Lee. Lee believed the town, founded in 1877, was destined to be the Colorado state capitol. He built a huge governor's mansion and outhouse of brick. Little remains today of Lee's dream except the post office and some kilns.

The steep-sided valley, coated with aspen and spruce forest, narrows and the road becomes rougher past Capitol City. Whitmore Falls, a couple miles past Capitol City, makes a good stop. A short path leads to a spectacular view of the falls and a rocky canyon. The road continues climbing, passing meadows, willow-lined beaver ponds, and creeks that cascade out of hanging valleys.

Rose's Cabin, an early stage stop, lies off the byway just below timberline. Corydon Rose built a twenty-two-room hotel and bar in 1875. By 1885 the site boasted a population of 120, a post office, smelter, store, and restaurant. The main building was torn down in 1950, leaving only the hotel fireplace and parts of the sixty-mule stable.

Passenger cars need to turn around at Rose's Cabin. This is a good place to shift into four-wheel-drive. The byway climbs above timberline, passing the remains of the Palmetto Gulch Mill, before turning up Palmetto Gulch. A narrow shelf road leads to the summit of 12,800-foot Engineer Pass, the byway's high point. Spectacular views abound from here, with jagged peaks cleaving the horizon in every direction.

The byway turns south from the pass and climbs up the west flank of 13,218-foot Engineer Peak. A short spur leads to a dramatic overlook to the west. The rocky road edges onto the exposed south face of the peak, its steep grassy slopes plunging away from the track. Keep your vehicle geared low and look for the occasional turnout. This section is slick when wet, use caution.

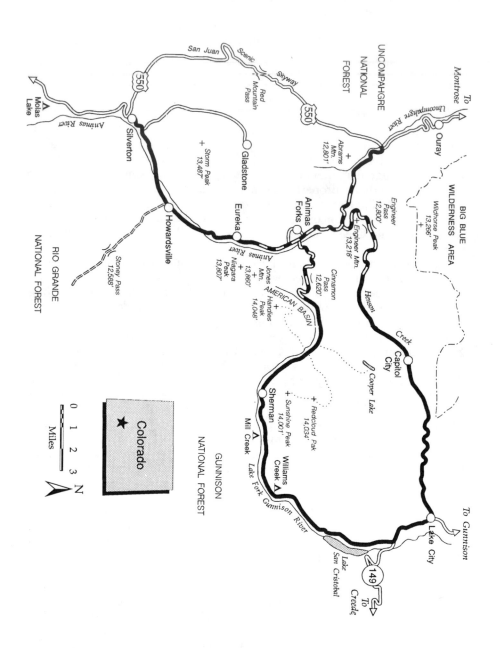

After two titillating miles of steep grades and switchbacks, the byway reaches grassy flats at Mineral Point. In the 1870s and '80s this was one of the area's busiest mining districts. The town, settled in 1873, had a summer population in the hundreds. It dwindled in the harsh winters, however, to a handful.

The byway spur to Ouray, nine miles away, turns west at Mineral Point. The road, for the first mile, is rough, muddy, and full of potholes. Further down it reaches timberline and switchbacks to Mineral Creek. Five miles down it turns north above the Uncompahgre River. Poughkeepsie Gulch, a hazardous jeep trail, turns south here and follows the river to beautiful Lake Como. Past the Mickey Breene Mine, the byway becomes a dramatic shelf road, creeping along the vertical edge of a deep box canyon. The road ends on U.S. 550 about two miles south of Ouray. Accommodations, camping, and other services are found in Ouray.

The byway also heads south from Mineral Point and travels three miles south along the North Fork of the Animas River to Animas Forks, one of Colorado's best ghost towns. Animas Forks, laid out in 1877, was located at the junction of the wagon routes from Silverton, Ouray, and Lake City. It was also the northern terminus of the Silverton Northern Railroad. In its heyday the town had a post office, school, newspaper, and railroad turntable. All that remains today at the 11,200-foot townsite are a few houses, foundations of the Gold Prince Mill, and the remains of the Columbus Mill which operated as late as the 1930s.

Silverton lies twelve miles down the Animas River from Animas Forks. The road drops down an impressive canyon that widens into a valley after five miles. The upper road is barely passable in a passenger car; the lower section is wide and graded. Along the byway a mile north of Eureka remains of a snowshed that once covered the railroad tracks can be seen. Eureka, another mining town, depended on the Sunnyside and other mines.

Howardsville, the first San Juan mining camp, was settled in 1872 by miner George Howard. The Pride of the West Mill still operates sporadically here. A jeep trail travels six miles southeast to 12,588-foot Stony Pass and the headwaters of the Rio Grande, and then on to Creede.

The byway continues to Silverton, passing old mines, mill ruins, tram lines, and the still-operating Mayflower Mill. Silverton, founded in 1873 in broad Baker's Park, is a well-preserved mining town. The famed Durango and Silverton Narrow Gauge Railroad ends in town. Silverton has visitor services, including campgrounds.

From Animas Forks the byway heads east three miles up a rocky shelf road toward 12,620-foot Cinnamon Pass. The first mile is steepest as the road edges along steep, grassy slopes. Higher, it climbs into a basin and switchbacks up to the pass summit. Here are magnificent views east to Redcloud, Sunshine, and Handies peaks, all over 14,000 feet.

The four-wheel-drive road twists down from the pass, reaching the Lake Fork of the Gunnison River in 2.5 miles. A turn to the south climbs into scenic American Basin. Mid-summer wildflower displays are spectacular in the basin. A short trail leads to Sloan Lake and then up 14,048-foot Handies Peak.

The byway, now easily passable to cars, heads down through Burrows Park, a wide valley lined with aspen, fir, and spruce forests and carpeted with green meadows. A good camping area is at the Silver Creek trailhead. The trail climbs north through a wilderness study area to the summits of 14,034-foot Redcloud Peak and 14,001-foot Sunshine Peak.

Snow-covered ponderosa pine branches on the Alpine Loop Byway near Lake City.

Beyond Silver Creek, the road drops steadily and becomes a winding shelf road. A wide valley and the townsite of Sherman is reached after five miles. A flash flood destroyed Sherman, established in 1875, after a dam broke above the town. The byway borders the Gunnison River, passing beaver ponds and thick aspen forests. Two campgrounds, Mill Creek and Williams Creek, lie alongside the route.

The byway passes Lake San Cristobal, Colorado's second largest natural lake. Two major mudslides that occurred 700 and 350 years ago dammed the river, forming the long lake. Past the lake the now-paved byway joins Colorado Highway 149 and drops two miles north to Lake City.

7 GOLD BELT TOUR
Colorado

General description: A 122-mile loop through scenic canyons on the southern slope of Pikes Peak between Cripple Creek and Canon City. It is a Type I and II byway, with some paved sections but mostly graded gravel roads.
Special attractions: Indian Springs Trace Fossil Site, Beaver Creek Wilderness Study Area, Victor National Historic District, Cripple Creek National

Historic District, Window Rock, Shelf Road Climbing Area, Garden Park Fossil Area, Red Canon Park, Skyline Drive, Canon City National Historic District, Royal Gorge Park.

Location: Central Colorado, southwest of Colorado Springs. The byway, three interconnecting roads that form a loop, begins in Florence on Colorado Highway 67 and travels north via the Phantom Canyon Road to Victor and Cripple Creek. Return can be by either Shelf Road or High Park Road to Canon City. U.S. Highway 50 passes through Canon City.

Byway route names and numbers: U.S. Highway 50, Colorado Highways 115, 67, and 9, Phantom Canyon Road, Shelf Road, and High Park Road.

Travel season: The byway is open year-round, although snow may temporarily close the unpaved portions during the winter.

Camping: Private campgrounds exist at both the Cripple Creek and Canon City ends of the byway. Primitive camping is allowed on public lands along the byway. National forest campgrounds are found in Pike National Forest north of the byway in Eleven Mile Canyon.

Services: All services are available in Canon City, Florence, Cripple Creek, and Victor.

Nearby attractions: Temple Canyon Park, Florissant Fossil Beds National Monument, Mueller State Park, Pikes Peak, Beaver Creek State Wildlife Area, Lost Creek Wilderness Area, Eleven Mile Canyon, Arkansas Headwaters Recreation Area, Colorado Springs, Lake Pueblo State Recreation Area, Pike National Forest, San Isabel National Forest.

For more information: Canon City District Office, 3170 East Main Street, P.O. Box 2200, Canon City, CO 81212. (719) 275-0631.

The Trip: The Gold Belt Tour Back Country Byway connects the Cripple Creek and Victor gold mining district with Canon City and Florence in the Arkansas River Valley via three unsurfaced roads. Two routes, Phantom Canyon Road and Shelf Road, slice south through steep canyons on the southern slopes of Pikes Peak. High Park Road crosses open mountain parklands.

The roads, linked by paved state and U.S. highway segments, are generally narrow and winding with frequent scenic pullouts. Trailers and motorhomes should not attempt to travel the Phantom Canyon Road and upper Shelf Road. Both narrow in places to one lane, hemmed in by canyon walls. High Park Road and lower Shelf Road, with two lanes, are accessible to larger vehicles. Driving time on each of the three segments is about two hours. Traffic is light, although Phantom Canyon can be very busy on summer weekends and holidays.

The weather in this area is generally moderate. Canon City boasts Colorado's mildest year-round weather. Summer temperatures range from the nineties in the Arkansas River valley to the seventies in the Cripple Creek region. Autumn temperatures are slightly cooler, but pleasant with generally clear skies. Winter and spring weather is more unpredictable, with frequent snowfalls and wind at the higher elevations.

The Gold Belt byway offers tremendous natural diversity, climbing almost 5,000 feet from its low point on the Arkansas River at Florence to almost 10,000 feet at Victor. The lower elevations are desert-like, with cholla and prickly pear cactus interspersed with shortgrass prairie. As you climb up through the canyons, you pass through pygmy forests of pinyon pine and juniper. Higher

The Arkansas River cuts through the Royal Gorge on the Gold Belt Tour Byway west of Canon City.

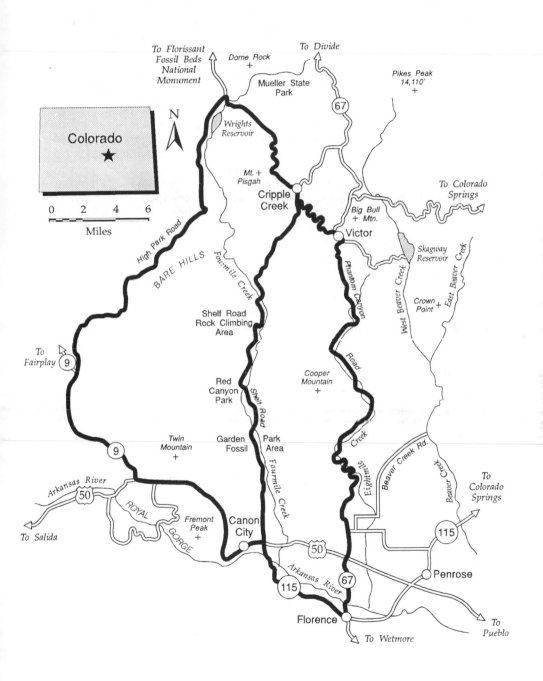

up are open ponderosa pine forests, and dense groves of fir and spruce on moist north-facing slopes. Along the byway between Cripple Creek and Victor grow stands of quaking aspen that are particularly colorful in late September.

The byway begins in Florence just south of U.S. 50 along the Arkansas River. Florence was a boom town in the 1890s after the first railroad to the Cripple Creek gold camp was pushed through Phantom Canyon. At its height the town had nine reduction mills for processing gold ore. Today, it's a peaceful ranching and farming center. The byway heads north from Florence following Colorado 67 across U.S. 50 and into Phantom Canyon.

The Phantom Canyon Road, traversing the abandoned railroad bed of the Florence and Cripple Creek Railroad, "The Gold Belt Line," crosses dusty cholla cactus-studded plains north of U.S. 50 before passing through a notch in an abrupt Dakota sandstone hogback. Past the hogback lies Indian Springs Trace Fossil Site, a National Natural Landmark containing the 460-million-year-old trails and burrows of ancient arthropods. The winding road continues up a narrow cliff-lined canyon, through two railroad tunnels and past glades of aspen and wildflowers, to Victor, the "City of Mines."

The 26,150-acre Beaver Creek Wilderness Study Area adjoins Phantom Canyon on the east. It's a rugged mountainous region, cleaved by deep canyons and lorded over by granite cliffs. Beaver Creek is prime wildlife habitat for peregrine falcons, black bears, bighorn sheep, cutthroat trout, and one of Colorado's largest concentrations of mountain lions. A trailhead at the historic steel bridge offers access to Beaver Creek from Phantom Canyon.

Victor lies on the slopes of Battle Mountain at the southern end of the Cripple Creek Mining District. The Gold Coin Mine, one of the district's greatest gold producers, operated within Victor, while the mountainside above was covered with famous mines—the Ajax, Portland, and the fabulously wealthy Independence. Still a mining town, Victor has been designated a National Historic District. Victor's most famous native is celebrated at the Victor-Lowell Thomas Museum. The town sponsors Gold Rush Days every July.

From Victor, the Gold Belt Tour continues on paved Colorado 67 to Cripple Creek. The winding road passes remains of the 500 mines that once operated in the district and the Carlton Mill that currently removes gold from old mine tailings. This byway stretch offers spectacular views of the snowcapped Sangre de Cristo Range seventy miles southwest.

Cripple Creek, sister city to Victor, was the financial and social center of the mining district. In 1890, Bob Womack, a forty-six-year-old cowboy, found the first traces of gold in aspen-filled Poverty Gulch above today's Cripple Creek. He called his claim the El Paso Lode. Hence began the nation's last great gold rush. When it was over, miners had extracted almost 500 million dollars and twenty-one million ounces of gold ore—more than the combined total of both the California and Alaska gold rushes. Now a National Historic District, Cripple Creek offers a wealth of activities for visitors, including tours in the Mollie Kathleen Mine, train trips on the Cripple Creek & Victor Narrow Gauge Railroad, the Cripple Creek District Museum, and the Old Homestead Museum, the last of the old "parlor houses" or brothels that once lined the town's red light district.

Byway travelers have two options to pick from for the return trip to the Arkansas Valley—Shelf Road and High Park Road. Shelf Road, an historic stage route to Cripple Creek, connects Cripple Creek with Canon City. The road follows Cripple Creek itself down a steep rocky canyon. Window Rock, a

The Cripple Creek and Victor Narrow Gauge Railroad steams away from Cripple Creek along the Gold Belt Tour Byway.

unique granite arch, towers over the narrow byway. Bighorn sheep frequently graze among the cliffs above the road. Further down, Shelf Road's most spectacular section traverses shelf-like across a steep mountainside leaving nervous drivers white-knuckled. Far below the road, Four-Mile Creek tumbles over smooth benches of granite. The road also passes Shelf Road Climbing Area, offering some of the world's finest limestone rock climbing, and Red Canyon Park, with hiking trails and picnic tables. Just north of Canon City, the byway passes through Garden Park Fossil Area, where colorful Morrison Formation outcroppings yield dinosaur bones, including the world's first stegasaurus skeleton.

High Park Road joins Colorado Highway 9, west of Canon City, with Cripple

A coiled rattlesnake near Phantom Canyon on the Gold Belt Tour Byway.

Creek. The byway crosses more open country than its two companions, traversing tawny meadows and open ponderosa pine woodlands. Pikes Peak and the Sangre de Cristo Range are seen from the road. It passes through traditional cattle grazing country. Mule deer are often sighted along the road. High Park Road also provides access to Florissant Fossil Beds National Monument, Mueller State Park, and Mt. Pisgah.

The Arkansas River, south of the Gold Belt's U.S. Highway 50 segment, slashes through an ancient plateau carving a deep, narrow canyon—the Royal Gorge. The gorge, a Canon City park, boasts the world's highest suspension bridge, measuring 1,053 feet from the bridge deck to the canyon bottom. River rafters plunge through twenty miles of foaming, frothy cataracts in the canyon, making the Royal Gorge one of the West's most thrilling boat rides. Other rafting opportunities as well as outstanding trout fishing are available upstream from the gorge in the Arkansas Headwaters Recreation Area, a 148-mile river park managed jointly by the Bureau of Land Management and the Colorado Division of Parks and Outdoor Recreation.

The Gold Belt Tour ends at Canon City, the largest city along the byway, just below the Royal Gorge. Founded in 1860, Canon City was home to Colorado's first territorial prison in 1868. The downtown is a national historic district. Visitors can tour the city's museums and celebrate its fruit industry during Blossom Days in May.

Pasque flowers, a harbinger of spring, sprout from scrub oak leaves alongside the Gold Belt Tour Byway.

General description: A 101-mile, Type I byway that crosses high plateaus, canyons, and mountains in southwestern Idaho.

Special attractions: North Fork of the Owyhee River Canyon, Owyhee Mountains, hiking, camping, picnicking, hunting, scenic views, fishing, solitude, wildlife.

Location: Southwestern Idaho along the Oregon border. The byway's eastern access is just east of Grand View on Idaho State Highway 78. The western access is in Jordan Valley, Oregon from U.S. 95.

Byway route name: Deep Creek-Mud Flat Road.

Travel season: June through September. Heavy snow, beginning in October, closes the road until May. Check with the BLM for road conditions.

Camping: Primitive camping is allowed on BLM land along the byway. The North Fork Recreation Site, on the North Fork of the Owyhee River on the byway's western end, has seven campsites. Poison Creek Recreation Site, on the eastern end, has picnic facilities. Bruneau State Park, east of the byway, has a campground with showers.

Services: No services along the byway. Complete services are available at Grand View and Jordan Valley.

Nearby attractions: Leslie Gulch-Succor Creek Back Country Byway, Bruneau Dunes State Park, Snake River Birds of Prey Natural Area, Snake River, Boise area, Owyhee Wild and Scenic River, Silver City, Bruneau River, Oregon Trail, Owyhee Front OHV Management Area.

For more information: BLM, Boise District, 3948 Development Avenue, Boise, ID 83705. (208) 384-3300.

The Trip: The Type I Owyhee Uplands Back Country Byway traverses high desert mountains, plateaus, and canyons in far southwestern Idaho. Travelers see dramatic, far-reaching views into Oregon and Nevada from the byway and experience solitude in this remote region.

The one-and-a-half lane, gravel byway crosses generally flat or gently rolling topography, although steep road sections with grades up to twelve percent occur occasionally at plateau breaks. There are numerous pullouts for passing and scenic views. The road is easily driven in a passenger car during good weather. Snow closes the road from October into May. Check with the BLM office in Boise for current road conditions. Allow six to eight hours to drive the byway route.

Weather on the Owyhee Uplands is generally pleasant in summer, with highs between seventy and ninety. Down along the Snake River plain at the byway's eastern access, temperatures often climb into the low 100s. Rain and thunderstorms occur along the byway's upper elevations. Autumns are mild, with warm days and cool nights.

The byway begins two miles east of Grand View on Idaho State Highway 78. Take a turn to the south where the highway makes a wide turn. A BLM road sign points toward Mud Flat and Juniper Mountain. The first thirteen miles are paved as the byway passes farms and ranches. Brilliant fields of

Horses graze on a fertile pasture along the Owyhee Uplands Byway.

cultivated sunflowers brighten the roadside during August.

After a few miles the plowed bottomlands give way to bare, rounded hills studded with desert shrubs. Slowly the road curves southwest through broad dry washes and across an outwash plain covered with sagebrush toward the low Owyhee Mountains. The byway enters Poison Creek canyon after eighteen miles.

The byway climbs steadily alongside Poison Creek. The creekbed is thickly lined with willows, aspens, and poplars. Steep slopes, carpeted with sagebrush and short grass, rise on either side to high buttes rimmed with layers of rhyolite tuff. A small picnic area at Poison Creek Recreation Site sits midway up the canyon. Here the creek trickles through dense underbrush under the shadow of towering poplar trees. The picnic area is fenced to keep cattle out.

Five miles past the picnic area, the byway reaches a lofty divide. Tawny mountains slope up from the road. A good hike climbs south from the byway up a gradual hillside to the summit of a rounded mountain on the eastern flank of the Owyhee Mountain Range. Past the divide, the road rolls and dips along a high crinkled plateau, dissected by shallow swales filled with grass and basalt ridges, for almost thirty-five miles. Distant views to the south reveal snowcapped Jarbidge and Bull Run mountains in northern Nevada.

Traveling westward, sagebrush and grass slowly gives way to scattered woodlands of mountain mahogany. These small trees, with small, leathery leaves, is a favorite deer food. Their conspicuous seeds have a long, curled, hairy tail that helps implant the seed in soil. Further west, gnarled woodlands of western juniper dominate the ridgetops and dry rocky hillsides of the

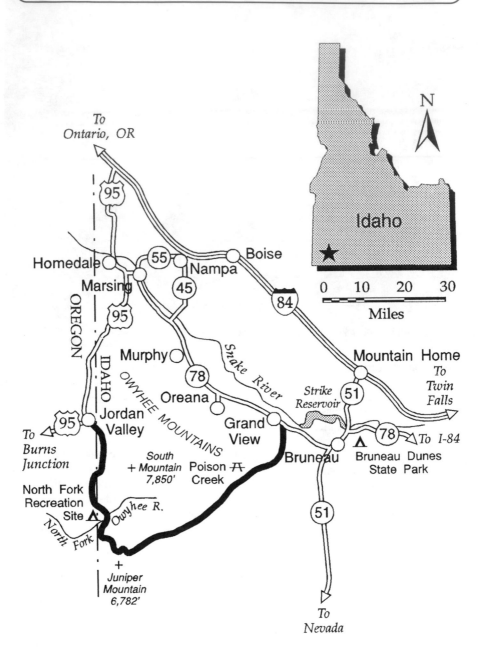

To
Ontario, OR

95

Homedale
Marsing
55
Nampa
Boise
45
84

OREGON
IDAHO
95

Murphy
Oreana
78
Snake River

Mountain Home
To
Twin
Falls

Strike
Reservoir
51

OWYHEE MOUNTAINS

Jordan
Valley
95
To
Burns
Junction

Grand
View
Bruneau
78
To I-84

North Fork
Recreation
Site

South
+ Mountain
7,850'
Poison
Creek

Bruneau Dunes
State Park

North Fork
Owyhee R.

51

+
Juniper
Mountain
6,782'

To
Nevada

N

Idaho
★

0   10   20   30
Miles

dissected plateau. South Mountain rises to the north above the plateau. Some junipers here reach ages of 300 years. Pastures of sagebrush, grass, and wildflowers cover the deep soils of shallow valley floors. The BLM uses prescribed burns and woodcutting to maintain these areas for grazing cattle and foraging wildlife. Pockets of quaking aspen grow on moist hillsides, and provide splotches of color in September.

After passing Juniper Mountain, the byway turns north a few miles east of the Oregon border and traverses the rimrock of a narrow, cliffed canyon. The road drops down onto the eastern edge of an expansive flat plateau that stretches west into Oregon. To the west, the long ridge of Steens Mountain rises over this vast expanse of desert in southeastern Oregon broken only by the abrupt gorges of the Owyhee River and its tributaries. Heading north, the road parallels a rhyolite escarpment. Numerous steep-walled canyons, including Cottonwood Creek, cut through the dark wall of cliffs.

The North Fork of the Owyhee River Canyon, the best scenery on the byway, comes suddenly. The road crosses a low ridge and edges down into the canyon. The small river runs glassy between gates of dark brown rhyolite. Soaring cliffs, spindly minarets and pinnacles, ribbed buttresses, and sharp aretes tower over the river as it winds downstream. The North Fork Recreation Site, with seven campsites and a restroom, nestles in the canyon bottom. This site is about seventy miles west of the byway's start and thirty miles south of Jordan Valley.

The Owyhee River and its many forks arise in the northern mountains of Nevada and flows northwestward in a broad arc through southwestern Idaho and southeastern Oregon to the Snake River west of Boise. This remote river cuts through a deep, forbidding gorge on its 200-mile journey through a high desert of crumbling sedimentary rocks overlaid by volcanic tuff and flows. The river, the mountains, and the byway are named for three luckless Hawaiian trappers brought to America in 1819 by the Hudson Bay Company. The trio vanished in southwestern Idaho, massacred by Indians. Their memory is now linked to the region with the name Owyhee—an early misspelling of Hawaii. The North Fork of the Owyhee in Idaho is currently being studied for inclusion in the Wild and Scenic River system. The Owyhee River system in Oregon is a National Wild River.

The byway climbs sharply out of the canyon and heads north along the Oregon and Idaho stateline over low hills, rounded ridges, and valleys covered with grass and sagebrush. The west flank of South Mountain towers over the road. The byway passes wide, well-watered pastures and hay fields and occasional ranch houses. Dropping into the green valley of Jordan Creek, the byway becomes paved. It bends west into Oregon and ends in the picturesque community of Jordan Valley. A right turn on U.S. 95 leads north eighteen miles to the start of the Leslie Gulch-Succor Creek Back Country Byway. Interstate 84 is about sixty miles northeast of Jordan Valley.

General description: A thirty-nine-mile-long, Type I byway that climbs up to Lemhi Pass where Lewis and Clark crossed the Continental Divide in 1805.
Special attractions: Lewis and Clark National Historic Trail, Continental Divide National Scenic Trail, Lemhi Pass, Sacajawea Memorial (Beaverhead National Forest, Montana), Salmon National Forest, hiking, wildlife, camping, snowmobiling.
Location: On the Idaho and Montana border twenty miles south of Salmon. The byway is accessed on the west by Idaho Highway 28 at Tendoy. Eastern access is on Montana State Highway 324 west of Interstate 15.
Byway route numbers: U.S. Forest Service Roads 185 and 013.
Travel season: June through October. Heavy snow closes the byway from November through early June.
Camping: A primitive BLM campground with toilets but no potable water is about five miles up Agency Creek from Tendoy on the Lemhi Pass road.
Services: Limited services at Tendoy, otherwise all services at Salmon twenty miles north.
Nearby attractions: Medicine Lodge-Big Sheep Creek Back Country Byway, Beaverhead National Forest, Salmon River, Lewis and Clark State Historic Site (Montana), Clark Canyon Recreation Area (Montana).
For more information: BLM, Salmon District Office, Highway 93 South, P.O. Box 430, Salmon, ID 83467. (208) 756-5400.

The Trip: The Lewis and Clark Back Country Byway climbs from Tendoy along the Lemhi River to the crest of the Continental Divide and Lemhi Pass on the Idaho and Montana border. Lemhi Pass is where the Lewis and Clark Expedition crossed from the newly acquired Louisiana Purchase over the Continental Divide into the unclaimed Pacific Northwest in 1805. The byway traverses a wide variety of terrain, including bare slopes covered with grass and sagebrush, thick forests of lodgepole pine along the divide, and the deep canyon of Agency Creek.

The byway makes a loop that begins and ends at Tendoy, a roadside stop named for a famed Shoshone chief. The gravel road is mostly single lane, but has numerous pullouts and passing areas. The road can be safely driven in a passenger car in good weather. There are some very steep grades, particularly the last two miles that edge up to Lemhi Pass. Remember that uphill vehicles have the right-of-way. The byway is closed by snowpack from November through early June. Check with the Salmon BLM office for the road condition in June and October. Allow three hours to drive the byway.

Summer and autumn weather along the byway is widely variable. Expect daily highs between fifty and eighty degrees, with cool nights. Heavy thunderstorms are common in August and snow can fall anytime in September and October. Winters are extremely cold. Parts of the byway are groomed during the winter for snowmobile use.

The Lewis and Clark Byway begins at Tendoy, twenty miles south of Salmon on Idaho Highway 28. The byway loop can be traveled in either direction.

LEWIS AND CLARK

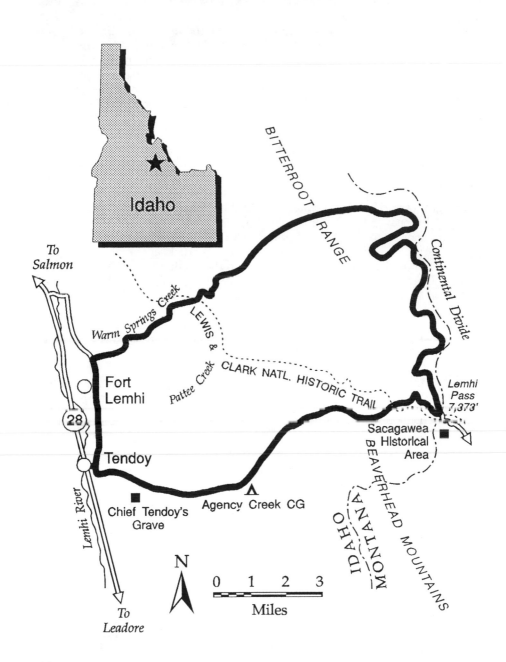

Idaho

To
Salmon

BITTERROOT RANGE

Continental Divide

Warm Springs Creek

LEWIS &

Pattee Creek

CLARK NATL. HISTORIC TRAIL

Fort
Lemhi

28

Tendoy

Lemhi River

Chief Tendoy's
Grave

Agency Creek CG

Lemhi
Pass
7,373'

Sacagawea
Historical
Area

BEAVERHEAD MOUNTAINS

IDAHO

MONTANA

N

0   1   2   3

Miles

To
Leadore

The best way to travel it if you plan to return to Highway 28 is to turn north just past Tendoy. The wide gravel road runs north, passing fertile pastures and ranch homes on the Lemhi River floodplain.

After almost three miles, the byway passes the site of Fort Lemhi. This religious settlement, built in 1855 by twenty-seven Mormon missionaries, was to instruct the local Indians in "the art of husbandry and peace according to our Gospel plan." The remote outpost had over 100 inhabitants before it was abandoned in 1858. The departing Mormons did, however, leave the name Lemhi from King Limhi in the Book of Mormon on the river and mountain pass. Today, a few adobe walls from the old fort remains in the grassy paddock. This is private property and visitors need to obtain permission before entering the fort's site. Sacajawea, the famed Shoshone interpreter of the Lewis and Clark Expedition, was born nearby.

MacDonald's Battle occurred just north of here in 1823. Hudson Bay trapper Finnan MacDonald and fifty-one men were camped along the river when they were ambushed by a group of Blackfeet Indians. They "fought like demons" before the trappers gained the upper hand by setting fire to the brushy thicket where the Blackfeet were hidden. The inferno flushed out the warriors and sixty-eight were killed. MacDonald later said he wouldn't trap this valley again unless "the beaver will have a gold skin."

The byway turns up Warm Springs Road after three miles (U.S. Forest Service Road 185) and begins ascending the rounded sagebrush- and grass-covered mountain flanks. The road turns up the shallow valley of dry Warm Springs Creek and after another mile heads north around a barren slope. Higher, the byway crests atop a grassy ridge crossed by the Lewis and Clark National Historic Trail. An historical marker here commemorates the spot where the American flag was first unfurled west of the Continental Divide. On August 13, 1805 Meriwether Lewis approached three Shoshone Indians "on an eminence immediately before us . . . when we had arrived within half a mile of them I directed the party to halt and leaving my pack and rifle I took the flag which I unfurled and advanced singly towards them." There are splendid views of the Lemhi and Salmon river valleys from this high vantage point.

The road continues steadily climbing past the historic marker, and after two miles the bare sagebrush and grass slopes yields to a Douglas fir forest in Salmon National Forest. Far below, Pattee Creek tumbles down a steep canyon. Heading east, the road eventually joins up with the creek as it placidly meanders through meadows and beaver dams.

The byway turns south along the winding Continental Divide sixteen miles from its start at Tendoy. The ten-mile byway section from here to Lemhi Pass is part of the 3,100-mile-long Continental Divide National Scenic Trail from Mexico to Canada. Hikers, backpackers, mountain bikers, and byway travelers share the road as its threads through dense stands of lodgepole pine. The road, winding in and out of ridges below the Divide crest, offers tantalizing glimpses of sharp mountain ranges edging the Idaho skyline. The byway leaves the forest behind for the last two miles to Lemhi Pass and drops down steep grassy hillsides to the pass.

Lemhi Pass is one of America's great historical spots. This is where Captains Meriwether Lewis and William Clark and their Corps of Discovery first crossed the Continental Divide on their epic exploration of the Louisiana Purchase and the Oregon country. The expedition, dispatched by President Thomas

The Continental Divide towers over the Lewis and Clark Byway near the site of old Fort Lemhi.

Jefferson in 1804, was to travel up the Missouri River, find passage over the great divide, and float down the Columbia River to the Pacific Ocean. Their intent was to find a navigable waterway to the Pacific, establish a trade route to the Far East, secure a slice of the rich fur trade, and lay title to the unclaimed northwest.

Lewis and Clark and their thirty-odd men and one woman had traveled fifteen months from St. Louis by the time they reached the divide. Lewis and an advance party crossed 7,373-foot Lemhi Pass, a low, well-traveled Indian route over the Beaverhead Range in search of the Shoshone bands Sacajawea had told them would be encamped in the river valley on the western side.

On August 12, 1805 Lewis stood atop the pass and gazed west at a tangle of formidable mountains. The view today is unchanged from 1805. High mountains, rimmed by snowfields, march across the Idaho horizon. Deep valleys, coated with forest and grassland, drop steeply below the road. Just south of the pass summit in Montana is a small picnic area and a memorial to Sacajawea, "Bird Woman", who traveled with her infant son, French husband Charboneau, and the Corp of Discovery to the Pacific. Interstate fifteen in Montana lies forty miles east of the pass. Sections of the road east of the pass are often muddy and rutted.

From the top of Lemhi Pass, the byway plunges west down Agency Creek Road (Forest Service Road 013). The route, for two miles, is a very steep, single-lane shelf road. Lower down, the road crosses Horseshoe Bend Creek where Lewis "first tasted the water of the great Columbia River." The road drops steadily down a deep canyon carved by Agency Creek. Seven miles from the pass is the primitive BLM Agency Creek Campground.

Before reaching Tendoy, the canyon widens and the byway passes some small ranches. Here at the canyon mouth is the grave of Chief Tendoy, a respected Shoshone chief who aided in the peaceful white settlement of Lemhi Valley. The grave, still visited by Lemhi Indians, is a sacred site. Visitation by the general public is considered inappropriate use. Respect their wishes and view the grave from the byway. Shortly beyond the cemetery the byway ends at Tendoy.

10 MISSOURI BREAKS
Montana

General description: A seventy-three-mile, Type II byway through the scenic Missouri Breaks along the Upper Missouri Wild and Scenic River in north-central Montana.

Special attractions: Upper Missouri Wild and Scenic River, Lewis and Clark National Historic Trail, Nez Perce National Historic Trail, Charles M. Russell National Wildlife Refuge, James Kipp State Park, camping, hiking, wildlife observation, canoeing, hunting, scenic views.

Location: North-central Montana. The byway's western access is twelve miles northeast of Winifred and Montana State Highway 236. The eastern access is from U.S. 191 just south of the Fred Robinson Bridge over the Missouri River.

Byway route names and numbers: Knox Ridge Road (BLM Road 0801 and Russell Wildlife Rufuge Road 209), Lower Two Calf Road (BLM Road 0815 and Russell Wildlife Refuge Road 307).

Travel season: May through October. Snow and mud close the roads during the winter and spring months.

Camping: James Kipp State Park on the east end of the byway has many sites with water and toilets. A primitive BLM is along the Missouri River at Woodhawk Bottom, accessible via the Woodhawk Bottom Road on the byway.

Services: Limited services are available in Winifred and at Mobridge, three miles south of James Kipp State Park. Complete services in Lewistown.

Nearby attractions: Judith Peak Recreation Area, Lewis and Clark National Forest, Little Rockies, Charles M. Russell National Wildlife Refuge, Lewistown, Central Montana Museum (Lewistown).

For more information: BLM, Lewistown District Office, 80 Airport Road, Lewistown, MT 59457. (406) 538-7461.

The trip: The Missouri Breaks Back Country Byway makes a seventy-three-mile-long loop drive along the scenic southern rim of the Upper Missouri Wild and Scenic River. Sweeping views unfold along the byway of the Missouri River in its shallow canyon, of distant forested mountains that punctuate the horizon, of colorful cliffs and badlands that drop away below the road. The byway also traverses a land rich in history, wildlife, and solitude.

The byway borders and parallels a segment of the 149-mile Upper Missouri Wild and Scenic River. During the 19th century, when it was called the Big

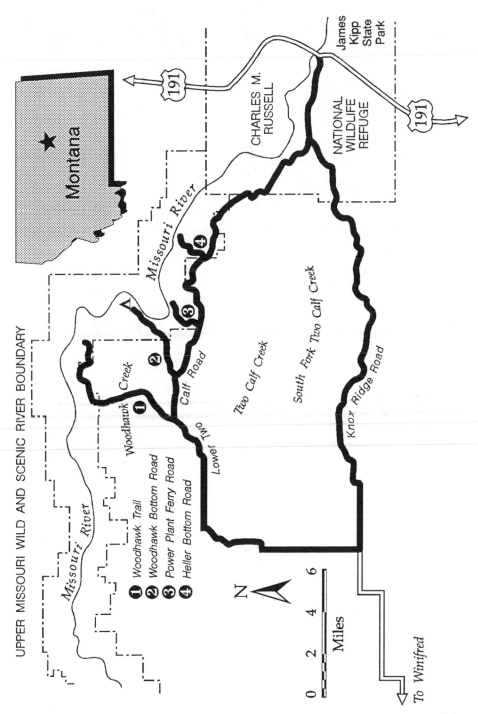

UPPER MISSOURI WILD AND SCENIC RIVER BOUNDARY

Montana

CHARLES M. RUSSELL

NATIONAL WILDLIFE REFUGE

James Kipp State Park

191

Missouri River

Woodhawk Creek

Calf Road

Lower Two

Two Calf Creek

South Fork Two Calf Creek

Knox Ridge Road

❶ Woodhawk Trail
❷ Woodhawk Bottom Road
❸ Power Plant Ferry Road
❹ Heller Bottom Road

N

Miles
0   2   4   6

To Winifred

51

Muddy and the Mighty Mo, the Missouri was a river of exploration, trade, and commerce. Since then the river has been dammed, channelized, and siphoned until this lonely river path across Montana's empty high plains remains as the last untamed section of the fabled 2,446-mile Missouri River. This is the last part of the river that remains as pristine as it was when Lewis and Clark labored up its strong, frigid current in the spring of 1805.

The Type II byway follows two roads—thirty-nine-mile Knox Ridge Road and thirty-four-mile Lower Two Calf Road—that make a loop drive between Winifred and James Kipp State Park on U.S. 191. Each road can also be driven one-way between the two points. A number of spur roads leave Lower Two Calf Road and drop down to the Missouri River bottom or to dramatic overlooks.

All the roads become impassable when wet, even after small amounts of moisture, and impassable to all vehicles. Do not attempt any byway sections that are wet or muddy. The byway can be safely driven in a passenger car during dry conditions. Small motor homes can also negotiate the byway but are not recommended for the roads within the wildlife refuge. Allow five or six hours to drive the byway.

Knox Ridge Road is a mostly two-lane, all-weather, gravel and dirt road except within Charles M. Russell National Wildlife Refuge. The refuge road section, about four miles long, has very steep grades just west of U.S. 191.

The Missouri River placidly meanders below the Missouri Breaks Byway.

The unsurfaced Lower Two Calf Road follows the rim of the breaks above the river. The grades on either side of Two Calf Creek are steep.

Weather along the byway from late spring through autumn is generally pleasant. Expect summer high temperatures to be between eighty and 100 degrees. Thunderstorms occur regularly in July and August. Be alert for changing weather conditions that might make the byway impassable. Autumn is characterized by mild days and cool nights.

The byway begins just south of the Fred Robinson Bridge over the Missouri River on U.S. 191. James Kipp State Park, named for a fur trader who established a trading post upriver in 1831, is along the river by the bridge. The park has numerous camping sites nestled among towering cottonwoods and a boat launching area.

The byway heads west on Knox Ridge Road, a single-lane dirt track, into the western end of 1,094,000-acre Charles M. Russell National Wildlife Refuge. The road, after one-half mile, climbs abruptly up a steep, narrow ridge of shale. The grey shale, called the Bearpaw formation, was deposited in an inland sea about seventy million years ago near the close of the Cretaceous Period. The shoreline of the sea as it retreated is called the Hell Creek formation and is renowned worldwide for its rich fossil lode. Fossil collecting for mollusks, including ammonites, baculites, clams, and oysters, is permitted on BLM land. The rarer vertebrate fossils like dinosaur bones are protected by law and must be left in place.

After three miles of steady climbing up the ridgeline, the byway flattens and widens out. Spectacular views spread out from the byway atop the Missouri Breaks. "Breaks" is the old term early pioneers called the eroded landforms along the river. The river valley, not severe enough to be called a canyon or gorge, "breaks" away from the undulating prairie above. French fur trappers called this Missouri section *Mauvaises Terres* or the "Bad Lands."

Four miles from U.S. 191 Knox Ridge Road reaches its eastern junction with Lower Two Calf Road. Turn right and follow Lower Two Calf Road northwest where it quickly descends to Two Calf Creek. The grade up the gully's west side is also very steep. Do not attempt the descent into Two Calf Creek if the road is at all muddy. Once atop the rim of the breaks, the byway meanders through tawny grasslands broken by ponderosa pine forests sprinkled across the steep north-facing slopes.

The entire length of Lower Two Calf Road offers excellent opportunities for seeing wildlife. Over sixty mammal species, 233 bird species, and twenty reptile and amphibian species inhabit the byway area. Elk, mule deer, and pronghorn antelope range across the area's fertile grasslands and shallow valleys. Rocky Mountain bighorn sheep, introduced in 1958 and 1961, are often sighted along the steep canyons below the road. The native Aububon bighorn sheep that originally roamed Montana was extinct by 1916. Other byway animals alert visitors might see include beavers, coyotes, prairie dogs, pheasant, sage grouse, sharp-tailed grouse, golden eagles, prairie falcons, and American kestrels. Bring binoculars for a close-up view of the watchable wildlife.

Continuing west, the byway leaves the wildlife refuge and enters BLM land. Two-mile-long Heller Bottom Road leaves the byway a few miles further on and winds down to the Missouri River bottom. Private land along the river is farmed for produce here. The muddy river, lined with stately cottonwoods and willows, is home to forty-nine species of fish. Fishermen catch walleye,

An abandoned farmhouse along the Missouri Breaks Byway weathers in the summer sun.

northern pike, channel catfish, carp, sauger, small mouth buffalo, and paddlefish that reach 140 pounds.

Five miles further east is the Power Plant Ferry Road. This two-mile road drops steeply down to the site of an old power plant that used water and coal to generate electricity for gold mines in the Little Rocky Mountains to the north. The Power Plant Ferry carried traffic across the river here until the bridge on U.S. 191 was completed in 1959.

Past the ferry road, the byway pulls away from the rim and crosses grassy swales and forested ridges. Another side road, the five-mile Woodhawk Bottom Road, goes down to the river, a small BLM campground, and the Gus Nelson Homestead. Swedish-born Gus Nelson homesteaded the river bottom in 1917 and farmed it for twenty-three years. Weathered cabins hunker all along the river bottoms and on the breaks above, remnants of a turn-of-the-century land rush that failed from floods, harsh winters, and insect infestations.

The Nez Perce National Historic Trail also follows the Woodhawk Bottom Road from rim to river and then north up Cow Creek. Chief Joseph and his Nez Perce band crossed the Missouri River here on September 23, 1877. The tribe, eluding the military to avoid reservation confinement, was fleeing to Canada. The Nez Perce asked for supplies at Cow Island Landing on the river here. Soldiers guarding the steamboat freight refused, so the Indians took what they wanted and burned the rest. They were captured on October 5, forty-five miles from the Canadian border.

The ten-mile Woodhawk Trail, two miles west of Woodhawk Bottom Road and twenty-four miles west of U.S. 191, runs north along the edge of the breaks above the Missouri. Sunshine and Deweese ridges, near the road's end above the river, offer dramatic views of the haunting badlands. Below are water-grooved hillsides, fluted ravines, sharp-edged ridges, and white bluffs that gleam in the sunlight. Meriwether Lewis wrote in 1805 that the breaks resembled "a thousand grotesque figures...ranges of lofty freestone buildings...vast pyramids of conical structure."

The byway leaves the breaks after Woodhawk Trail and heads southwest past rolling grasslands with grazing cattle and pronghorn, low scrubby mesas rimmed with rock outcrops and pines, and lonely ranch homes and wheat fields. Turning west and then sharply south the byway crosses ten miles of farmland to the junction of Lower Two Calf Road and Knox Ridge Road. Winifred, a picturesque ranch community, lies twelve miles west of the junction.

To complete the byway loop, turn east on Knox Ridge Road. The first couple miles cross wheat fields and an abandoned ranch. The rest of the byway to the eastern junction with Lower Two Calf Road, a distance of about twenty miles, rolls over a gentle prairie covered with sagebrush and grass. Shallow vales, filled with ponderosa pine, cut across the land toward the river. Wild-life abounds on this section. Herds of pronghorn antelope and majestic mule deer bucks roam the open spaces; a coyote dashes into tall grass alongside the road; and in fall, the trumpeting of elk ring across the hills.

Just past the junction with Middle Two Calf Road, the byway again enters the Charles M. Russell National Wildlife Refuge and again becomes a very rough, single-lane track for almost four miles to Lower Two Calf Road. U.S. 191 and the end of the byway lies four miles east from here.

11 BIG SHEEP CREEK
Montana

General description: A fifty-mile, Type I byway through scenic canyons and valleys in the Bitterroot Range and Tendoy Mountains in southwestern Montana.

Special attractions: Camping, hiking, fishing, scenic views, hunting, Lewis and Clark National Historic Trail.

Location: Southwestern Montana. The byway's southern access is twenty-four miles north of the Montana and Idaho state line at Dell on Interstate 15. The byway begins two miles south of Dell on the west frontage road. The northern access is on Montana State Highway 324 three miles west of Clark Canyon Dam and seven miles west of Interstate 15.

Byway route name: Big Sheep Creek/Medicine Lodge Road.

Travel season: The byway can be safely driven from May through October.

Camping: There is primitive camping along the byway on BLM land. There is a primitive BLM campground at Deadman Gulch in Big Sheep Canyon.

Services: Limited services at Dell. Complete services at Dillon forty miles north of Dell on Interstate 40.

Nearby attractions: Clark Canyon State Recreation Area, Beaverhead National Forest, Lewis and Clark Back Country Byway (Idaho), Lemhi Pass,

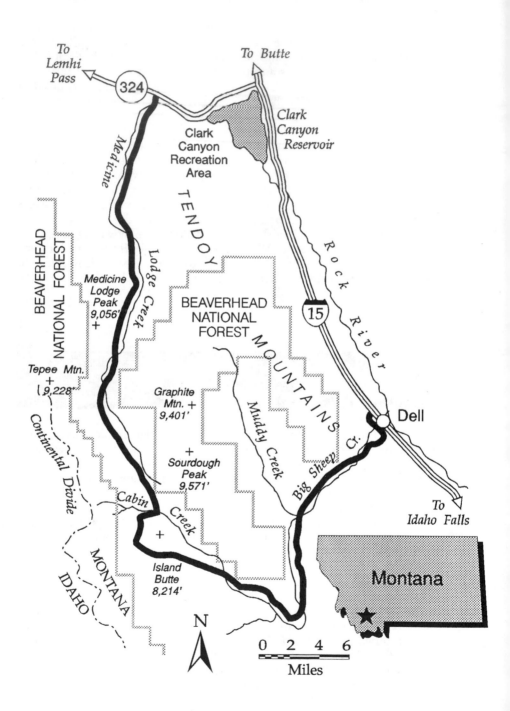

To
Lemhi
Pass

To Butte

324

Medicine

Clark
Canyon
Recreation
Area

Clark
Canyon
Reservoir

BEAVERHEAD

NATIONAL FOREST

T E N D O Y

Lodge Creek

Medicine
Lodge
Peak
9,056'
+

Tepee Mtn.
+
9,228'

BEAVERHEAD
NATIONAL
FOREST

M O U N T A I N S

Rock River

15

Graphite
Mtn. +
9,401'

Muddy Creek

Big Sheep Cr.

Dell

Continental Divide

+
Sourdough
Peak
9,571'

Cabin

Creek

+

To
Idaho Falls

MONTANA

IDAHO

Island
Butte
8,214'

Montana

N

0   2   4   6
Miles

Continental Divide National Scenic Trail, Lewis and Clark National Historic Trail, Bannack State Historic Park.

For more information: BLM, Butte District Office, 106 N. Parkmont, Butte, MT 59702. (406) 494-5059. Or Dillion Resource Area Office, P.O. Box 1048, Dillon, MT 59725. (406) 683-2337.

The trip: Big Sheep Creek-Medicine Lodge Back Country Byway makes an open fifty-mile loop through deep canyons and valleys separating the Bitterroot Range and the Continental Divide from the rounded Tendoy Mountains.

The Type I, gravel byway is mostly two-lane, although one section in Big Sheep Basin is single-lane. Travelers should beware of the substandard road section in upper Big Sheep Basin. This can be driven only by four-wheel drive vehicles early in the season and after heavy rains due to deep mud and ruts. Motor homes and vehicles with trailers should not attempt driving the entire route. Allow three or four hours to drive the byway.

Expect variable mountain weather along the byway during summer and autumn. Daily highs in these high valleys range between sixty and eighty degrees. Although in the rainshadow of the Continental Divide, heavy thunderstorms occur regularly in July and August. Snow can fall in September and October.

The byway begins off Interstate 15 at Dell. Drive two miles south on the frontage road west of the interstate and turn west on the marked byway road. The route heads west across the wide valley to a deep cleft in the southern Tendoy Mountains, a range named for a famed 19th century Shoshone Indian chief.

After a few miles the byway enters the deep, V-shaped canyon. Big Sheep Creek tumbles and rolls over cobbles and boulders beside the road. Overhead tower ragged cliffs and long scree slopes. Deadwood Gulch lies to the south near the end of this canyon section. The BLM maintains a small primitive campground here. Hidden Pasture, north of the road, is the site of the BLM's successful reintroduction of bighorn sheep to the Tendoy Mountains.

Past the five-mile-long canyon, the byway enters a wide park. Cattle graze in fenced pastures on river-bottom ranches. Muddy Creek Road, allowing access to the crest of the Tendoy Mountains, heads north from here.

Leaving the park, the road cuts straight south into a spectacular canyon carved by Big Sheep Creek. Tilted layers of ancient limestone form steep cliffs that overhang deep, clear pools in the creek. Excellent trout fishing is the biggest lure for visitors to the canyon. Juniper and sagebrush dominate the steep canyon walls. The byway, following Big Sheep Creek, eventually turns northwest and after a couple miles leaves the creek and heads up a barren canyon carved by intermittent Cabin Creek.

After three miles the byway abruptly leaves the canyon and its upturned limestone ridges and enters spacious Big Sheep Basin. This high, wide basin is flanked on the north and east by low rounded mountains and on the west and south by the snowcapped Bitterroot Range. The rolling grassland, with cloud shadows trailing across it, feels like the floor of the sky. Alert eyes and a pair of field glasses can often sight wildlife here, including elk, mule deer, pronghorn antelope, and moose. Birds seen are eagles, hawks, owls, and sage grouse.

The byway, continuing northwest along Cabin Creek, heads toward isolated 8,219-foot Island Butte, a prominent landmark in the northern part of the

The Big Sheep Creek/Medicine Lodge Byway plunges through a rugged canyon along Big Sheep Creek.

basin. After six miles across the basin and past the last ranch gate, the road becomes single-lane and rough. Rainwater collects in low marshy areas along the road and it becomes deeply rutted, muddy, and impassable to all but four-wheel-drive vehicles. It dries out during warm weather and is passable to passenger cars.

Forest Service Road 3917 turns west from the byway where it swings north near Island Butte. This road leads to Morrison Lake in Beaverhead National Forest. Continuing north, the byway passes an abandoned, overgrown ranch before dropping down and crossing Sawlog Creek. The road climbs steeply for 1.5 miles from the creek up grass- and sagebrush-covered slopes to a windy saddle that divides the Big Sheep Creek drainage from the Medicine Lodge Creek drainage.

The divide, mid-point on the byway, is a good place to stop and hike up the bare ridges on either side. Marvelous views of Big Sheep Basin and the Continental Divide stretch away from these rounded summits. The old Corrine Wagon Trail, a freight road between Corrine, Utah and Bannack, the site of Montana's first major gold strike in 1862 to the north, runs through this low pass. Grassy swales carved by the rolling wagon wheels are visible in places on both sides of the divide.

The byway drops north into scenic Medicine Lodge Valley. This gentle, open valley is flanked by rolling mountains dotted with groves of fir and aspen. The grassy floor is divided into ranches, pastures, and hayfields. The two-lane, graded road passes numerous peaks, including two tepee-shaped peaks—

9,228-foot Tepee Mountain and 9,056-foot Medicine Lodge Peak. As the byway heads north, the valley slowly widens and becomes drier. Forests cling only to the moist north-facing slopes and sagebrush colors the hillsides with a dull gray sheen. A rough side-road up Deer Canyon climbs east to the crest of the Tendoy Mountains.

The byway ends on paved Montana State Highway 324 after traveling twenty-six miles down Medicine Lodge Creek. Interstate 15 lies seven miles east of the junction, while Lemhi Pass and Bannock Pass sit on the Continental Divide to the west.

The Lewis and Clark National Historic Trail crosses the broad valley just north of the byway's end. One of the expedition's most dramatic events happened at Camp Fortunate Overlook, about a mile from Clark Canyon Dam and just east of the byway. On August 17, 1805 the explorers met with Shoshone chief Cameahwait in the shade of a tent. They sent for Sacagawea, a young Shoshone woman who had been captured by a neighboring tribe five years before, to interpret the conversation. Meriwether Lewis wrote: "...she came into the tent, sat down, and was beginning to interpret, when in the person of Cameahwait she recognized her brother. She instantly jumped up, and ran and embraced him, throwing over him her blanket and weeping profusely."

12 GARNET RANGE
Montana

General description: A twelve-mile, Type IV byway that climbs 2,000 feet by snowmobile and skis into the well-preserved ghost town Garnet in the Garnet Range east of Missoula. The town is also accessible by road the rest of the year.
Special attractions: Garnet, Coloma (ghost town), scenic views, cross-country skiing, snowmobiling, snowshoeing, picnicking, Garnet National Winter Recreation Trail.
Location: Far western Montana. Turn south into plowed parking areas at the Garnet byway trailhead between mile markers 22 and 23 on Montana Highway 200, about thirty miles east of Missoula.
Byway route name: Garret Karze Road.
Travel season: This winter recreation byway is marked and groomed by the BLM from January 1 through April 30. Garnet is easily accessible by car during good weather from May through October.
Camping: There is no camping along the byway. A couple of cabins in Garnet are available during the winter. Contact the BLM office in Missoula for information and reservations. In summer, campgrounds are located in nearby Lolo National Forest, Missoula, and along Interstate 90.
Services: All services are located thirty miles west in Missoula.
Nearby attractions: Lolo National Forest, Missoula, National Bison Range, Rattlesnake National Recreation Area and Wilderness Area, Ninemile Remount Depot, Fort Missoula.
For more information: BLM, Butte District Office, 106 N. Parkmont, Butte, MT 59702. (406) 494-5059; or BLM, Garnet Resource Area, 3255 Ft. Missoula Road, Missoula, MT 59806. (406) 329-3914.

The well-preserved ghost town of Garnet lies at the end of the Garnet Range Back Country Byway east of Missoula.

The trip: The Garnet Range Back Country Byway climbs 1,800 feet from Montana Highway 200 to the crest of the Garnet Range and the well-preserved ghost town of Garnet. The Type IV byway, designated for snowmobile and cross-country ski use, is part of the Garnet National Winter Recreation Trail system. The BLM maintains fifty-five miles of developed winter trails in the Garnet Range. A map of the trails is available at the BLM office in Missoula.

The byway, groomed and marked by the BLM from January 1 through April 30, follows the Garnet Range Road. The gravel, mostly two-lane road is easily driven by automobile in good weather from May through October. Road grades are gentle to moderate, with the steepest at ten to twelve percent. Beginning to intermediate snowmobilers and intermediate to advanced cross-country skiers can negotiate the trail with no problems. Only the main byway route from Montana 200 to Garnet is regularly groomed. Other side trails are groomed infrequently or not at all.

When traveling the byway in winter, be prepared for severe weather by listening to local forecasts. Be prepared for snow, whiteouts, high winds, and cold temperatures by wearing proper winter clothing. Protect exposed skin from frostbite by wearing gloves and headgear. Avoid hypothermia, the lowering of the body's core temperature, by carrying food, water, waterproof outer layers, and extra clothing. Hypothermia most often happens when the victim's clothes become wet from sweat, rain, or melting snow. Travel with at least two companions, leave information about your plans and destination, and stay on marked trails. Watch for cattle guards along fencelines, barbed

GARNET RANGE

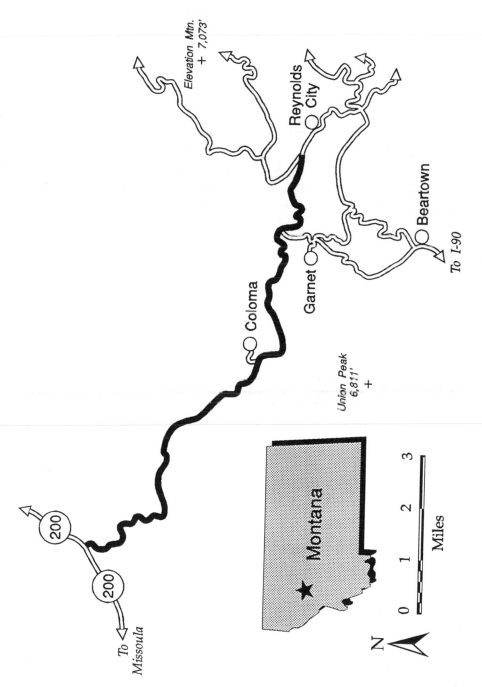

Elevation Mtn.
+ 7,073'

Reynolds
City

Beartown

To I-90

Coloma

Garnet

Union Peak
6,811'
+

200

200

To
Missoula

Montana

N

0   1   2   3
Miles

wire fences buried by drifting snow, and mine shafts hidden by snow.

Use courtesy and common sense on the byway. Skiers should allow snowmobilers to safely pass by moving to the side of the trail. Likewise, snowmobilers should respect skier's rights by slowing down. Some side trails are designated for skiers only. Respect the restriction. Avoid running over and damaging young trees in logged areas. Dogs should be kept in control to avoid stressing wintering animals and kept off of groomed trails.

Winter weather along the byway is severe, with extremely cold temperatures and heavy snowfall. Expect a daily temperature range from well below zero to the mid-thirties. Early spring temperatures in March and April can climb into the forties with sunny skies.

The byway begins twenty-two miles east of Interstate 90 and about thirty miles east of Missoula. Turn south on the Garnet Range Road and park in a plowed lot. The trail crosses a cattle guard and almost immediately begins climbing up the northern flank of the Garnet Range. The range and the town were named for the many garnets found in the area. For the first four miles the route travels through Lubrecht Experimental Forest, managed by the University of Montana in Missoula.

After seven miles, a short road leads north to the ruins of Coloma, an old mining town. Sand Park pioneer cemetery lies alongside the byway a half-mile past the turn and a warming shelter sits beside the road after another half-mile. Animals that winter in the Garnet Range area include deer, elk, and moose. Byway travelers should avoid stressing the animals by viewing from a distance. Snow, cold, and limited food weakens the wildlife making winter survival difficult.

Marvelous views to the north of the Rattlesnake Wilderness Area, Swan Range, and the Blackfoot River Valley open up past the shelter as the byway traverses a steep hillside above a clear-cut area. Past here, the byway narrows and drops down through thick forest to the turn to Garnet. A short road winds south through dense woods to the ghost town.

Garnet got its start in 1895 when Dr. Armistead Mitchell built a stamp mill in First Chance Gulch. The town, originally named Mitchell, grew up around the mill. Rich veins of gold ore were found in the hills around the town, including the Nancy Hanks Mine which yielded about $300,000 worth of gold. By 1898 almost 1,000 people called Garnet home. There were four stores, four hotels, two barber shops, three stables, thirteen saloons, a butcher shop, a doctor's office, a school with forty-one students, and about twenty operating mines.

The boom was shortlived. By 1905 most of the mines were abandoned and the population had dropped to barely 200. A 1912 fire razed much of Garnet's commercial district and by the 1920s the town had given up the ghost. Garnet revived briefly in the mid-1930s when gold prices jumped from $16 to $32 an ounce, but World War II intervened and the town was deserted again.

Today, Garnet is Montana's best-preserved ghost town through the efforts of the Bureau of Land Management and the Garnet Preservation Association. Vandalism, which has destroyed most of the West's ghost towns, has been avoided at Garnet. The town has a year-round BLM caretaker to slow the destruction. The Garnet Preservation Association helps fund the caretaker position, stabilizes old buildings, and staffs the town's visitor center. The visitor center, with historical displays, books, and information is open on weekends through the winter. Several cabins in the town are available for overnight stays in the winter. Contact the BLM office in Missoula for information and reservations.

Beyond the Garnet turn, the byway continues for another couple miles before dropping down to its end at Elk Creek Junction. A maze of snowmobile and ski trails reach out across the mountains from here, traveling up forested valleys and over high ridges. The BLM publishes a handy Garnet Winter Recreation Trails map that details all the routes.

13 RED ROCKS
Nevada

General description: A Type I, thirteen-mile, one-way, paved, open loop road through the spectacular Red Rock Canyon National Conservation Area nineteen miles west of downtown Las Vegas.

Special attractions: Hiking trails, backpacking, birdwatching, rock climbing, wildlife observation, photography, picnicking, scenic views, visitor center with interpretive displays.

Location: Southern Nevada, about nineteen miles west of downtown Las Vegas and sixteen miles west of the Las Vegas Strip on Charleston Boulevard (Nevada State Highway 159). Travelers should exit west from Interstate 15 at the Charleston exit. Another route leaves Interstate 15 on Nevada Highway 160, proceed west to the intersection with Nevada Highway 159 and drive north to Red Rock Canyon.

Byway route name: Red Rock Canyon Loop Drive.

Travel Season: Year-round. Spring and fall are the best times to visit with pleasant temperatures ranging from fifty to ninety. Summer is very hot, with temperatures soaring to 100 and above. Winters are generally mild, but can have cold and windy periods with snow on the byway.

Camping: No camping along the byway loop. There is primitive camping in Red Rock Canyon National Conservation Area just south of the byway at the Oak Creek Canyon entrance. Inquire at the BLM Red Rock Visitor Center for more information. There are several campgrounds in Toiyabe National Forest in the mountains north of Red Rock Canyon. There are also numerous private campgrounds in the Las Vegas area.

Services: All services are available in Las Vegas.

Nearby attractions: Las Vegas Strip, Las Vegas Museum of Natural History, Old Mormon Fort, Nevada State Museum, Spring Mountain Ranch State Park, Floyd R. Lamb State Park, Hoover Dam, Lake Mead National Recreation Area, Valley of Fire State Park, Toiyabe National Forest, Gold Butte Back Country Byway, Bitter Springs Trail Back Country Byway.

For more information: Las Vegas District Office, 4765 W. Vegas Drive, P.O. Box 26569, Las Vegas, NV 89126. (702) 646-8800. The Red Rock Canyon Visitor Center's telephone number is (702) 363-1921.

The trip: The one-way, paved byway makes a thirteen-mile-long open loop around the perimeter of a desert basin rimmed on the north and west by

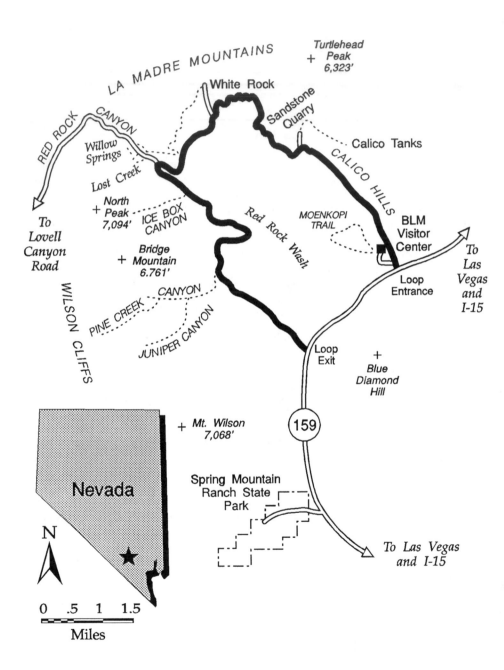

LA MADRE MOUNTAINS

Turtlehead
+ Peak
6,323'

White Rock

Sandstone
Quarry

RED ROCK CANYON

Willow
Springs

Calico Tanks

CALICO HILLS

Lost Creek

North
+ Peak
7,094'

ICE BOX
CANYON

Red Rock Wash

MOENKOPI
TRAIL

BLM
Visitor
Center

To
Lovell
Canyon
Road

Bridge
+ Mountain
6.761'

To
Las
Vegas
and
I-15

Loop
Entrance

PINE CREEK CANYON

WILSON CLIFFS

JUNIPER CANYON

Loop
Exit

+
Blue
Diamond
Hill

159

Nevada

+ Mt. Wilson
7,068'

N

Spring Mountain
Ranch State
Park

To Las Vegas
and I-15

0   .5   1   1.5

Miles

towering cliffs and rugged mountains. The well-maintained road has eight pullouts that offer grand scenery and spectacular views. Traffic, except on weekends, is generally light. The byway is open during the warmer months from 8 a.m. to dusk; in winter the hours vary with the length of the days.

Weather along the byway is mild in spring and fall, with daily temperatures ranging from fifty to ninety. Summers are hot. Expect highs over 100. Winters are pleasant with warm days and cold nights. There can be periods of light snow or rain.

The BLM Visitor Center, at the start of the byway, is the best place to start your drive. Inside are exhibits that detail Red Rock Canyon's geology, natural history, and history. Maps, brochures, books, and handouts are also available. The center is open daily from 9 a.m to 4 p.m.

The byway climbs northwest from the Visitor Center toward the Calico Hills, a scenic outcrop of Aztec sandstone domes seamed by narrow, redrock canyons. Two overlooks provide great views of the hills. Short trails begin at each overlook, leading down across a wash and into the hills. In spring you can find small pools of water among the rocks, vital drinking holes for the area's forty-five mammal species. The Red Rock Canyon region teems with wildlife, including wild burros, bighorn sheep, kit fox, coyote, mule deer, and bats. Cooler temperatures than the surrounding desert, forty natural springs, and a diversity of plants in the deep canyons provides ideal habitat for animals.

A good 2.5-mile hike to Calico Tanks begins at Sandstone Quarry, at the western end of the Calico Hills. The trail follows a wash north and east to a large tinaja or natural water tank. This and other pools in the bedrock fill with rainwater and are often brimming with insect larvae and fairy shrimp.

Continuing up the byway, the road offers spectacular views west of the Wilson Cliffs, a long escarpment of towering 180-million-year-old sandstone walls formed when the region was a vast dune field that extended from here eastward into Colorado. The cliffs are a direct result of the Keystone Thrust Fault, one of the world's best examples of a thrust fault where one section of the earth's crustal plates is thrust horizontally over another. The younger sandstone formations were "overthrust" by 600-million-year-old limestone and dolomite formations some fifty million years ago in a shift of the earth's crust. Hence the older rocks rest directly above the youngest rocks.

At the byway's mid-point, a short spur road leads to Willow Springs Picnic Area in steep-walled Red Rock Canyon. The spring seeps from under a sandstone overhang above the road. Nearby are several Indian roasting pits, including one of the largest in southern Nevada. Dependable water sources along the cliff escarpment made this area attractive to Indians as early as 3500 B.C. Indian cultures that lived here included the Anasazi, Patayan, and southern Paiute. Examples of Indian rock art are found on dark sandstone walls in Red Rock Canyon. Remember that all cultural artifacts are protected by federal law. Red Rock Canyon is also a popular rock climbing area.

An excellent 2.5-mile round-trip hike scrambles into Ice Box Canyon, a deep gorge sliced into the escarpment. At the trail's end lies a seasonal waterfall, steep, heavily-varnished cliffs, thick vegetation, and cool temperatures. It's a good hike for a hot day. This area is another favorite spot for climbing.

The last stop on the byway is the Pine Creek Canyon overlook. Along the rippling creek below grows a rare pocket of ponderosa pine, perhaps a relic grove of the large pine forest that covered this area after the last ice age some

The soaring sandstone walls of North Peak tower over Red Rock Canyon Back Country Byway.

10,000 years ago. Normally, they grow thousands of feet higher atop the mountains west of the byway. A two-mile round trip trail leaves the overlook, passes the old Wilson homestead, and follows Pine Creek into a soaring cliffed canyon filled with bird song and wind.

The byway drops away from the mountains at Pine Creek and wanders over a wide outwash plain studded with Joshua trees before emerging onto Nevada Highway 159 a few miles southwest of the Visitor Center.

GOLD BUTTE
Nevada

General description: A Type II, sixty-two-mile paved, gravel, and unmaintained road that traverses an area of stunning desert scenery in southeastern Nevada.

Special attractions: Whitney Pockets, Devil's Throat, Joshua tree forests, excellent views, Gold Butte mining area, wildlife, hiking.

Location: On BLM lands south of Mesquite and Interstate 15 in southeastern Arizona. The drive begins on Nevada Highway 170 five miles southwest of Mesquite and Bunkerville, and about seventy-five miles northeast of Las Vegas.

Byway route name: Gold Butte Road.

Travel season: Year-round, although fall and spring with their pleasant temperatures ranging from fifty to ninety degrees are the best times. Be prepared in summer for temperatures over 100 degrees. Plan on carrying plenty of water, both for yourself and your radiator. The BLM urges caution when traveling on the unmaintained section of road; in the event of a breakdown it could be days before another vehicle passes. Be sure and let someone know your travel plans.

Camping: Primitive camping is allowed along the byway. The best places are at Whitney Pockets and Gold Butte. Commercial camping is at Mesquite.

Services: All services are available at Mesquite, including motels, restaurants, groceries, and gas.

Nearby attractions: Lake Mead National Recreation Area, Bitter Springs Back Country Byway, Red Rock Canyon Back Country Byway, Mt. Wilson Back Country Byway, Valley of Fire State Park, Zion National Park, Las Vegas.

For more information: BLM, Las Vegas District Office, 4765 W. Vegas Drive, P.O. Box 26569, Las Vegas, NV 89126, (702) 646-8800. A detailed byway map is available on request.

The trip: Gold Butte Back Country Byway traverses sixty-two miles of rugged desert country south of Interstate 15 and Mesquite in southeastern Nevada. The byway is paved for the first twenty-four miles, with another nineteen miles on a well-graded gravel road to Gold Butte, an historic mining area at the southern end of the byway. Beyond there, the byway follows another nineteen-mile stretch that can be traveled only in a four-wheel drive or high clearance two-wheel drive vehicle. The byway takes between three and six hours to drive, depending on how many stops are taken and if the unmaintained section is driven.

Fall and spring are the ideal times to drive the Gold Butte Byway, with pleasant daytime temperatures ranging from fifty to ninety degrees. Summer is prohibitively hot, you can expect temperatures to climb to 100 degrees and above almost every day. If you do drive the byway in summer, be prepared. Carry lots of water for yourself and your radiator and bring a working jack and spare tire. If you are stranded, it is best to wait for a passing vehicle, or for those you notified of your trip plans to contact local authorities when you are overdue.

The byway begins just south of Interstate 15 on Nevada Highway 170 on

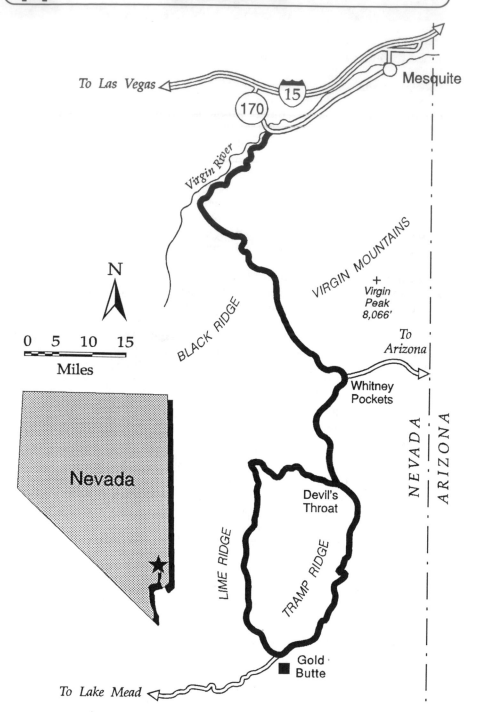

To Las Vegas

Mesquite

15

170

Virgin River

VIRGIN MOUNTAINS

+ Virgin Peak 8,066'

To Arizona

BLACK RIDGE

N

0 5 10 15

Miles

Whitney Pockets

Nevada

NEVADA

ARIZONA

Devil's Throat

LIME RIDGE

TRAMP RIDGE

Gold Butte

To Lake Mead

the south side of Virgin River bridge, or five miles west of Mesquite. The narrow paved road follows the Virgin River southwestward along tawny benchlands above the broad river valley. Tamarisk trees, an Asian import, thickly border the riverbanks. The byway travels through a patchwork of private and public lands along this section. Respect private property by crossing it only with the owner's permission.

After a few miles the road swings away from the river and crosses a wide creosote-covered bajada or outwash plain sloping west from towering Virgin Peak. The jagged 8,066-foot-high peak, centerpiece of the Virgin Mountain Natural Area, rises almost 6,000 feet above the byway. The road continues climbing away from the river and over Black Ridge, a low spur of the Virgin Mountains that reaches toward Lake Mead.

Forests of Joshua trees, a tree-sized yucca in the lily family, line the road as it swings east toward the Virgin Mountains. The further south you travel on the byway, the denser the Joshua tree forests. On the bajadas, close to the mountains, where sufficient moisture exists it is the dominant plant. As you drive away from the mountains to lower elevations, the Joshua trees become smaller and fewer until they are replaced by creosote. The yucca trees, popular symbol of the Mojave Desert, were christened by early Mormons. Captain John C. Fremont, however, called them "the most repulsive tree in the vegetable kingdom."

After twenty-four miles the byway curves around the south end of Virgin Peak into Whitney Pockets, a dazzling valley of red and buff-colored sandstone outcrops. This hard fine- to medium-grained sandstone, called Aztec Sandstone, was deposited 180 million years ago in a large dune field that blanketed parts of Colorado, Utah, Arizona, and Nevada. The area, named for a pioneer rancher, offers excellent primitive campsites and is a good place to see desert wildlife.

Some of the animals seen include turkey vultures, prairie falcons, desert bighorn sheep, golden eagles, Mojave rattlesnakes and sidewinders, great horned owls that nest in the rock formations, and the rare desert tortoise, state reptile of Nevada. Visitors should exercise extreme caution when hiking around the area's cliffs and boulders; rattlesnakes are present.

Beyond Whitney Pockets, the gravel byway drops south between Bitter Ridge and Wechech Basin over a plain studded with Joshua trees. Dramatic views of lofty Tramp Ridge lie straight ahead, while to the southwest glistens the deep blue of Lake Mead in the sunlight. Long, hazy mountain ridges in nearby Arizona punctuate the eastern sky.

On the flat below Tramp Ridge, the byway divides. The seventeen-mile, non-maintained section of the road leads west around Tramp Ridge. If you don't have a four-wheel drive or high-clearance vehicle, it is inadvisable to travel that section of the byway. There are both rocky and sandy sections that cannot be driven safely in a passenger car.

It is well worth the effort though, to take a quarter-mile jaunt down the road to Devil's Throat, an impressive, yawning sinkhole that is over 100-feet wide and deep. Expanding sinkholes are very rare in this area. Keep outside the fence around Devil's Throat. It is constantly eroding, with undercutting along the hole's rim just below the surface.

From Devil's Throat, the rough byway segment continues west along Mud Wash before turning south up Gold Butte Wash. Lime Ridge, a proposed wilderness area, lifts its ragged scarp above the track. Primitive camping and hiking opportunities exist along this wild section of road.

A Joshua tree frames Tramp Ridge on the Gold Butte Byway.

From the road junction at Devil's Throat, the graded gravel road climbs south to the now-abandoned and badly vandalized town of Gold Butte. This road section is spectacular. Dramatic vistas unfold in every direction: Virgin Peak's rocky profile zig-zags across the northern horizon, eastward lies row upon row of wild Arizona mountain ranges, to the west looms the abrupt folded uplift of Tramp Ridge, and southward are shapely granite peaks. Thick Joshua tree forests border the byway as it ascends Horse Spring Wash.

Gold Butte, halfway point of the byway journey, lies in the shadow of rough granite outcrops south of the road. Gold was discovered in 1905. By 1908, the town boasted a store, post office, hotel, and stable. Little gold and silver was extracted from the desert here, but copper was abundant. Nothing remains of Gold Butte today, except the traces and tailings of the Gold Butte Mine,

Hill Top Mine, Black Jack Mine, and Vermiculite Mine. A branch road continues southwest from Gold Butte another ten miles to the shores of Lake Mead.

Primitive campsites are all along the byway. The best places are at Whitney Pockets and around Gold Butte. Use proper camping etiquette by packing out all your trash, using established sites, and camping at least 600 feet from a water source. There is plenty of desert hiking along the road—every desert peak looks inviting. Hikers and campers need to carry enough water for all their needs, especially in the warmer months, and to be alert for rattlesnakes around rock outcrops and in bushes. Visitors should be aware that all archaeological and cultural resources are protected by federal law. Leave the artifacts and ruins of the Anasazi and Paiute Indians who once lived here intact for future byway travelers.

15. BITTER SPRINGS
Nevada

General description: A twenty-eight-mile, rough, single-lane Type II byway requiring a high-clearance or four-wheel drive vehicle that twists through the rugged Muddy Mountains between Interstate 15 and Lake Mead in southeastern Nevada.

Special attractions: Mojave desert landscape, outstanding views, abandoned borax mine, backcountry hiking, primitive camping.

Location: Southeastern Nevada near Lake Mead National Recreation Area, forty-five miles east on Interstate 15 from Las Vegas. The byway begins 4.5 miles east on the Valley of Fire State Park Road, Nevada Highway 40, and ends on Nevada Highway 12.

Byway route name: Bitter-Spring Trail.

Travel season: Year-round. Fall, winter, and spring temperatures are very pleasant, usually between forty and ninety degrees. Summer is very hot, be prepared for daily temperatures in excess of 100 degrees and may reach 120 degrees. Carry sufficient water and survival gear; a breakdown on this road leaves you far from the main highways and it may be awhile before another vehicle passes. Let someone know your travel plans before heading out.

Camping: Primitive camping is allowed along the byway. Good spots are Color Rock Quarry, Buffington Pockets, and Hidden Valley. Two campgrounds with fifty sites, shaded tables, water, showers, and restrooms are located at nearby Valley of Fire State Park. Other campgrounds are at Overton Beach and Echo Bay at Lake Mead National Recreation Area.

Services: All services are available at Overton Beach, including motels, restaurants, groceries, and gas.

Nearby attractions: Lake Mead National Recreation Area, Valley of Fire State Park, Las Vegas, Gold Butte Back Country Byway, Red Rock Canyon Back Country Byway.

For more information: BLM, Las Vegas District Office, 4765 W. Vegas Drive, P.O. Box 26569, Las Vegas, NV 89126. (702) 646-8800. A detailed map and brochure is available from the office.

The Bitter Springs Trail Byway follows a dry wash through the Muddy Mountains.

The Trip: The Bitter Spring Trail traverses a lonely section of the rugged Muddy Mountains, traveling across wide plains, through narrow canyons, and past old mining operations. The byway is narrow and rough. A four-wheel drive or high-clearance vehicle is necessary to follow the byway's entire length. Allow three or four hours to drive the route.

Spring and fall are the best times to drive the road. Temperatures are pleasant, with clear skies the norm. April and May also bring showy flower displays, with desert marigold, desert mallow, beavertail cactus, and prickly pear cactus spreading a colorful carpet across the drab desert floor. Winter is cooler but mild, with occasional rain and snow showers dusting the peaks. Summer is prohibitively hot. Summer temperatures do not vary widely from day to night, many nights don't drop below 90. Much of the region's average precipitation of four inches falls in a few summer thunderstorms. Don't travel the byway in the face of inclement weather, the road follows canyon bottoms subject to flash flooding.

The Bitter Spring Trail begins almost five miles south of Interstate 15 on Nevada Highway 40 to Valley of Fire State Park. Drivers should take the Valley of Fire exit about forty-five miles east of Las Vegas. The byway bumps south along a wide creosote-covered outwash plain. After four miles, a spur road turns right and climbs abruptly into a steep canyon and Color Rock Quarry. Sharp, barren peaks surround this picturesque spot, and side-canyons invite exploration.

Returning to the main route, the byway climbs into and follows a rocky canyon bottom to Buffington Pockets, a spectacular area of Aztec sandstone crags. The sandstone, deposited some 150 million years ago, was part of a huge, shifting dune field that covered most of Utah and parts of Arizona, Colorado, and Nevada. Good sites for primitive camping are found along the road here.

Winding up through the sandstone, the byway quickly reaches Hidden Canyon, a deep, boulder-strewn canyon. A short hike up it reveals colorful sandstone windows, spires, and buttresses. This off-the-beaten-track canyon is delightful. The Anasazi Indians, who frequented this area of Nevada from 1 A.D. to about 1150 A.D., also found it unusual. They left traces of their passing, a gallery of rock art, on the canyon walls. Walk up through the boulders and you'll find their petroglyphs carved into the soft sandstone, perhaps a magical plea for a good hunt. Archaic hunters and gatherers also lived in this area for the past 5,000 years. The Paiutes are the probable descendants of these ancient Indians.

Traveling around a high spur of the Muddy Mountains, the road drops into White Basin. To the south looms Muddy Peak, high point of the range. The byway forms much of the northern and eastern boundary of the Muddy Mountain Wilderness Study Area.

The remote basins and mountains along the road form outstanding habitats for desert wildlife. Visitors can glimpse many animals, including coyote, kit fox, skunk, blacktailed jack rabbit, wild horses, burros, desert tortoise, turkey vulture, roadrunner, and sidewinder rattlesnake. Wildlife biologists are also working to expand the range and population of the rare desert bighorn sheep in the area.

The trail follows dry graveled washes eastward to the remains of the American Borax Mine. Alongside mine tailings lie the mill's foundation, building remnants, thirty-foot-deep water cisterns, mine tunnels, and adits or horizontal passages carved into the hillsides.

East of the mine the byway traverses a steep-walled canyon that slices through Bitter Ridge, an eight-mile-long tilt fault. Emerging from the canyon, the fault scarp's vertical south face towers hundreds of feet over the road. For the last few miles, the byway drives through Echo Wash, past tamarisk and mesquite.

There are great views east of indigo Lake Mead and the desert ranges that line its shore. The last point of interest is Bitter Spring. It's water seeps out of the ground among thick stands of feathery tamarisk, before disappearing again in the sandy creekbed. The byway ends on paved Nevada Highway 12, just south of the turn to Lake Mead's Echo Bay.

A good return trip to Interstate 15 is via Valley of Fire State Park in a broad valley on the north side of the Muddy Mountains. This scenic area of brilliantly-colored sandstone formations has a fifty-site campground, picnic areas, and hiking trails. Visitors can also camp at Lake Mead National Recreation Area's Echo Bay and Overton Beach campgrounds just off Nevada Highway 12.

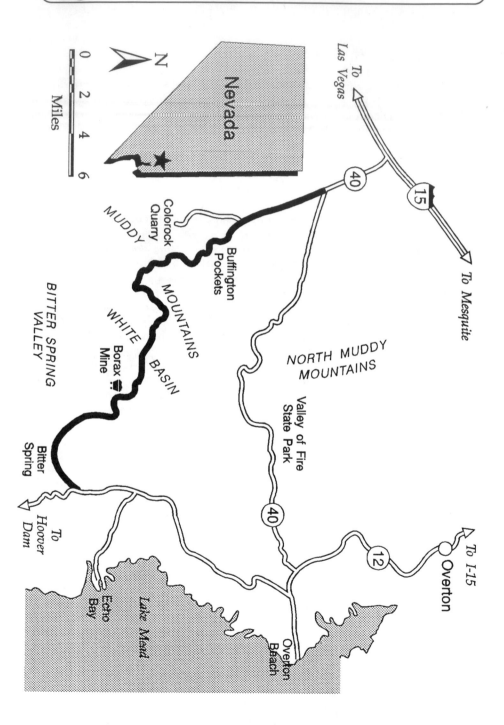

Nevada

N

Miles
0 2 4 6

To Las Vegas

15

40

To Mesquite

Colorock Quarry

MUDDY

Buffington Pockets

MOUNTAINS

WHITE

BASIN

NORTH MUDDY MOUNTAINS

Valley of Fire State Park

BITTER SPRING VALLEY

Borax Mine

Bitter Spring

To Hoover Dam

40

12

To I-15

Overton

Echo Bay

Lake Mead

Overton Beach

General description: A Type II byway that forms a sixty-two-mile-long open loop around Mt. Wilson in eastern Nevada.

Special attractions: Scenic views, hiking, trout fishing, Spring Valley State Park, pioneer cemetery, historic ranch buildings, camping.

Location: East-central Nevada near the Utah border. The byway leaves U.S. Highway 93, the Great Basin Highway, at Pony Springs twenty-nine miles north of Pioche, and ends via Nevada Highway 322 at Pioche.

Byway route numbers: Nevada Highway 322, Lincoln County Roads 430, 431, 440, and 441, and BLM Road 4045.

Travel season: May through October. Snow closes the route in the winter, and the road is often muddy from snowmelt until late April.

Camping: Primitive camping is allowed on BLM lands along the byway at already existing campsites. There are two established campgrounds along the byway at Spring Valley State Park and Meadow Valley Wash BLM Campground. No hookups.

Services: All services are in nearby towns including Pioche and Panaca. There are limited services along the byway at Ursine.

Nearby attractions: Great Basin National Park, Lehman Caves, Cathedral Gorge State Park, Echo Canyon State Recreation Area, Beaver Dam State Park, Gold Butte Back Country Byway.

For more information: BLM, Ely District Office, Star Route 5, Box 1, Ely, NV 89301. (702) 289-4865.

The trip: The Mount Wilson Back Country Byway climbs over a remote mountain range in eastern Nevada. It crosses wide basins, threads up narrow canyons, passes historical cabins and a pioneer cemetery, and offers fishing, hiking, and camping.

The byway begins twenty-nine miles north of Pioche in east-central Nevada on U.S. Highway 93, the Great Basin Highway, between Las Vegas and Ely. Pony Springs, the byway starting point, lies about ninety miles south of the visitor center at Great Basin National Park. Pony Springs is a pleasant point to embark on the byway. Tall cottonwoods shade picnic sites and a well provides cold water for your radiator in summer. The byway takes about four hours to drive.

The byway opens when the road clears of snow and mud in May through late October when snow closes its upper reaches. Summer visitors can expect pleasant temperatures on the byway, with daytime highs between seventy and ninety degrees. Nighttime temperatures are cooler, depending on elevation.

The byway's first ten miles lead eastward across broad Lake Valley, passing herds of grazing cattle. On hot summer days the forested slopes of Mt. Wilson ahead beckon visitors with the promise of cool mountain breezes. After crossing dry Patterson Wash, the road enters a scrubby pinyon pine and juniper forest and begins climbing, via Lincoln County Road 440 and then BLM Road 4045, up the steep western flank of the Wilson Creek Range.

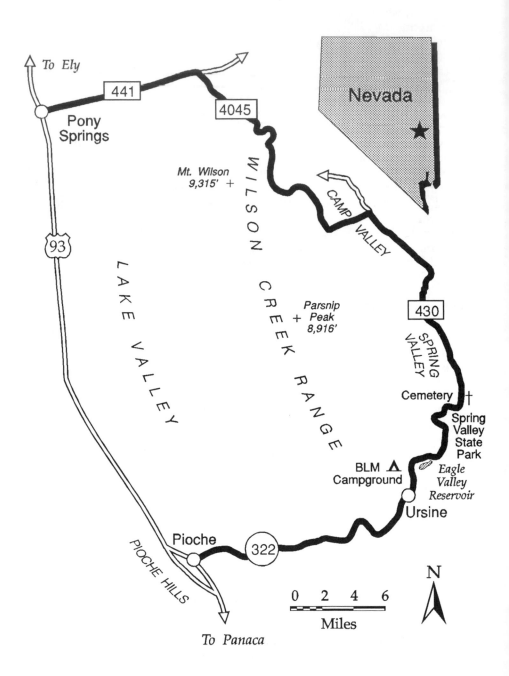

To Ely

441

Pony
Springs

4045

Nevada

Mt. Wilson
9,315' +

WILSON

CAMP VALLEY

93

LAKE VALLEY

WILSON CREEK RANGE

Parsnip
Peak +
8,916'

430

SPRING VALLEY

Cemetery †

Spring
Valley
State
Park

BLM △
Campground

Eagle
Valley
Reservoir

Ursine

PIOCHE HILLS

Pioche

322

To Panaca

N

0   2   4   6
Miles

As you climb, a remarkable variety of ecosystems characterized by various plant types are encountered. Down in Lake Valley you passed through the Upper Sonoran Zone, a high, dry desert of sagebrush, cactus, rattlesnakes, and jackrabbits. Ascending the Wilson Creek Range, you enter a transition zone of pinyon pine and juniper, a pygmy forest that spreads across the lower mountainsides. Many of the area's animals frequent the transition zone, passing between mountain and plain. Commonly seen animals include the ubiquitous mule deer, squirrels, coyotes, hawks, vultures, and various lizards. Visitors may also see wild horses along the byway.

After climbing steeply up a shallow canyon, the rough, narrow road winds along the range crest for several miles. This spectacular section offers scenic views north toward Great Basin National Park. Snowcapped Wheeler Peak, one of Nevada's highest points at 13,063 feet, gleams like an alabaster tower in the bright sunlight some seventy miles away. Unusual woodlands of mountain mahogany, a favorite deer food, manzanita, and fir border the byway.

A pulloff at the road's high point gives a great view of 9,296-foot Mount Wilson. Cornices of winter snow rim its rounded summit. Meadows of green grass broken by ponderosa pine and white fir forests and pockets of quaking aspen spill down its steep northern slope to Wilson Creek. Wildflowers dot the byway's upper elevations in summer, while autumn brings colorful leaf displays.

From here the byway drops abruptly down shallow canyons on the range's eastern side, passing the reclaimed 10,000-acre scar from the 1974 Mt. Wilson fire. Further down, the byway follows a wide, well-graded road through pastoral Camp Valley. The wide valley, bordered by undulating hills on the east and Parsnip Peak Wilderness Study Area in the Wilson Creek Range on the west, is a flood plain covered with grass and cattle.

Just before the byway enters Spring Valley it passes Spring Valley Cemetery, burying place of the region's earliest pioneers. Gravestone inscriptions in the rustic cemetery have slowly faded, while sagebrush has grown over its wrought iron fences. The valley's first settlers were Mormons who came in 1864. A permanent settlement and fort were established down-canyon in 1865.

Past the cemetery, the byway wends through lush Spring Valley. Along the roadside are picturesque stone ranch houses and eroded outcroppings of pink volcanic tuff. The byway follows Meadow Valley Wash downstream to where the canyon walls tighten and steepen. Here, hemmed in by cliffs, lies sixty-five-acre Eagle Valley Reservoir, the focal point of Spring Valley State Park. Anglers can try their luck for brown and rainbow trout and Alabama striped bass in its sparkling waters. Nearby is a twenty-two-site campground with showers and a picnic area. Below the dam, the byway threads down a steep-walled canyon past Meadow Valley BLM Campground to the historic town of Ursine.

From Ursine, the byway enters more open country covered with pinyon and juniper before crossing an expansive sagebrush plain and climbing up to the byway's end at U.S. 93 in Pioche. Between 1870 and 1873, Pioche was one of the West's toughest mining camps. The silver lodes in the hills west of town brought droves of miners and troublemakers. Over forty murders were committed in Pioche's first five years alone. The town is best known for its "million dollar courthouse." The building's construction debt was compounded by public officials stealing and carelessly borrowing money from

Graves of early pioneers lie in Spring Valley Cemetery on the Mount Wilson Byway.

the courthouse fund until the county's obligation was almost a million dollars. This town landmark and the opera house are both listed on the National Register of Historic Places. The remains of other mining towns surround Pioche, including Jackrabbit, Treasure Hill, Bristol Well, and Bullionville.

17 CALIFORNIA TRAIL
Nevada

General description: A Type I, seventy-six-mile open loop that parallels sections of the historic California Trail in northeastern Nevada.

Special attractions: California Trail, Mammoth Ruts, Rock Spring, rockhounding, camping, hunting, picnicking, wildlife viewing, solitude, scenic vistas.

Location: Northeastern Nevada, north of Interstate 80. The byway's southern access is twenty-six miles north of I-80 and Wells at the Thousand Springs turnoff on U.S. Highway 93. The northern access is two miles south of Jackpot on U.S. 93 just south of the Idaho border.

Byway route numbers: Elko County Roads C761, C762, C763, and C765.

Travel season: May through November. Snow and mud makes the road impassable from December through April.

Camping: Primitive camping on BLM land along the byway.

Services: All services are available at Wells and Jackpot. No services along the byway.

Nearby attractions: Humboldt National Forest, Jarbidge Wilderness Area, East Humboldt Wilderness Area, City of Rocks, Snake River, Ruby Mountains.

For more information: BLM, Elko District Office, 3900 E. Idaho Street, P.O. Box 831, Elko, NV 89801. (702) 738-4071.

The trip: The California Trail Back Country Byway makes an open loop through the wide open spaces of northeastern Nevada, crossing rolling sagebrush-covered hills and broad valleys, and traversing a countryside rich in American history. Part of the byway parallels the path of the old California Trail, the principal route to the California gold fields in the 1840s and 1850s, and the Magic City Freight Line between Toano, Nevada and Magic City, now Twin Falls, Idaho.

The Type I, gravel and dirt byway is passable to passenger cars. Three different trips are possible on the byway: Thousand Springs to Utah stateline (sixty-three miles); Thousand Springs to Jackpot (seventy-six miles); and Jackpot to Utah stateline (forty-nine miles). Most of the road is two-lane, but parts of the northern section on Elko County 761 narrow down to a single lane;

The Mammoth Ruts, deep grooves eroded by countless wagons in the 1840s and 50s, lie alongside the California Trail Byway.

it's impassable after heavy rain and from December through April due to snow and mud. The route travels through a very remote area. Be prepared for emergencies by having a full gas tank, plenty of water and food, and sleeping bags. Allow four to five hours to drive the byway.

Summers are generally dry and warm in the high desert of northern Nevada, with daily temperatures between eighty and 100 degrees. There are occasional afternoon thunderstorms. Vegetation can become extremely dry along the byway, take care with fire. Autumn temperatures often climb as high as ninety degrees, but it can be much cooler and stormy.

The byway begins twenty-six miles north of Wells and Interstate 80 on U.S. Highway 93 at the Thousand Springs turnoff. A wooden sign for the Wine Cup Ranch spans the road. The road heads east and northeast along the northern edge of wide Thousand Springs Valley, a popular stopping place for emigrant parties to water and pasture their livestock in the grassy meadows. Barren, rounded mountains rise north of the byway.

After fifteen miles a long ridge rimmed with broken crags rears up south of the dry valley. Look for a small metal marker among the clumps of sagebrush and saltbrush south of the road. This marks the Mammoth Ruts, a section of the California Trail worn as much as six feet below the valley floor.

The Mammoth Ruts is a good place to stop and reflect on the Forty-niners. Behind them lay almost 1,300 miles and three months of prairie and mountain travel along the Oregon Trail from Missouri. Just a few days back they had split off from the Oregon Trail at Idaho's City of Rocks and headed southwest along the Raft River and rugged Goose Creek into today's northeastern Nevada. Their wagons, pulled by teams of oxen or mules, creaked down Thousand Springs Valley along today's byway toward Wells and the sinuous 400-mile-long path of the Humboldt River, which provided important water and forage vital to the emigrant trains in arid Nevada.

The California Trail section along the byway was relatively easy traveling. The grades were gentle, there was firewood and game, and there was water. Two important springs, Rock Springs and Emigrant Springs, along the byway were popular camping spots for the pioneers. One 1849 Argonaut passing through here in mid-July described the route: "Our road, dusty, congested with ox-teams in the narrow pinches, and showing at every step the breaking-up of outfits, leads from Goose Creek through hills of sand covered with sage and greasewood . . . and opens to our vision a land where not a living thing is to be seen except here and there a demented lizard or a half-witted horned toad."

About six miles past the Mammoth Ruts, the byway turns north up Rock Spring Creek on Elko County Road 763. Mud Springs sits beside the roadside almost three miles from the junction, its soft banks trampled by cattle. One emigrant, after hurrying past the spring, said it was filled with decaying, bloated cattle.

The valley begins to narrow as the byway heads northeast. A juniper-clad mountain range edges the valley on the east. Rock Springs, an emigrant campsite, lies alongside the byway here. This was the first water the emigrants reached that drained into Nevada's Great Basin. The spring forms a shallow pool surrounded by boulders, low cliffs, and grass. Remnants of a saloon at a stage stop on the Magic City Freight Line are nearby. The abandoned homestead east of the road was built after the turn of the century.

The dusty byway rolls north up a narrow canyon and into a wide sagebrush-

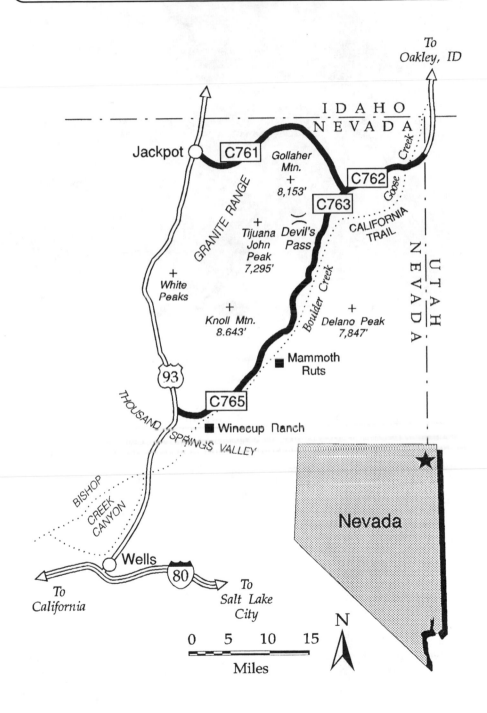

Rock Springs, on the California Trail Byway, was a popular campsite and watering hole for pioneers on the California Emigrant Trail.

covered valley broken by low rocky ridges dotted with scattered junipers. The road eventually drops down and splashes through Little Goose Creek. The byway divides here. Elko County Road 762 heads east eight miles to Goose Creek to rejoin the California Trail, and a few miles beyond that to the Utah stateline. The well-maintained road continues to Oakley, Idaho and the City of Rocks area. If you drive this spur you can also head back to the junction and then go north on Elko County 761 to complete the loop drive. This byway junction lies forty-five miles from its start back at Thousand Springs; Jackpot, the northern terminus, is thirty-two miles northwest.

The byway climbs north up a wide ridge to a pass at Summit Springs on the Deadline Ridge. The hills and rounded mountains surrounding the road are low and barren, covered with grey sagebrush. The pass offers a good view of 8,153-foot Gollaher Mountain, green with pockets of aspen in its high ravines. The road drops down into another wide valley that gently slopes northward.

Where the byway crosses Milligan Creek in the valley floor, a jeep road turns north to Rogerson, Idaho. A half-mile up the road lies a beautiful spring gushing out of the hillside and spilling into shallow pools lined with thick grass and wildflowers. This tiny oasis in the midst of the sagebrush desert is alive with birds, and hoofprints in its mud tell of the comings and goings of deer and pronghorn antelope. It's a good place to stop and look across a lonely, unspoiled landscape.

The byway slowly swings northwest then west as the road skirts the southern edge of the broad Shoshone Basin along the Nevada and Idaho border. It dips in and out of shallow valleys carved by small trickling creeks and passes cattle grazing on sagebrush and short grass. Gollaher Mountain, with sloping shoulders and barren slopes, rises south of the byway. Past Cedar Creek, the road drops into a valley and quietly ends on U.S. 93 about two miles south of Jackpot.

18 FT. CHURCHILL to WELLINGTON
Nevada

General description: A sixty-seven-mile Type I and II byway that travels along the Pony Express Trail from Fort Churchill to Dayton, climbs over the Pine Nut Mountains, and crosses wide Smith Valley to Wellington.

Special attractions: Pony Express Trail, Fort Churchill State Historic Monument, Dayton State Park, Como Mining District, Alkali Lake Wildlife Management Area, Dayton, Wellington, Pine Nut Mountains, scenic views, hiking, wildlife, camping, hunting, four-wheel driving.

Location: Western Nevada. The byway begins at Fort Churchill, thirty-five miles west of Carson City via U.S. 50 and Alternate U.S. 95. Fort Churchill is twenty-four miles south of Fernley and Interstate 80 on Alt. U.S. 95. Wellington, the southern terminus, is forty-eight miles south of Fort Churchill on Nevada Highway 208. It is also reached from Carson City via U.S. 395 and Nevada 208.

Byway route names and numbers: Nevada State Highway 2B, Como Road, Sunrise Pass Road, Upper Colony Road.

Travel season: Year-round on the lower sections of the byway. The route over the Pine Nut Mountains is impassable during the winter.

Camping: Fort Churchill State Historic Monument has a twenty-site campground shaded by cottonwood trees along the Carson River. Dayton State Park has a ten-site campground along U.S. 50 just east of Dayton. Primitive camping is allowed on BLM lands along the byway.

Services: Complete services are available at Dayton, Carson City, and Fallon. Limited services are at Wellington.

Nearby attractions: Carson City, Lake Tahoe, Virginia City, Reno, Churchill County Museum (Fallon), California Trail, Toiyabe National Forest, Sierra Nevada, Yosemite National Park, Lahontan State Recreation Area.

For more information: BLM, Carson City District, 1535 Hot Springs Road, Suite 300, Carson City, NV 89706-0638. (702) 882-1631.

The trip: The Fort Churchill to Wellington Back Country Byway traverses a rough land in Nevada's far western reaches; a land rich in history, beauty, and diversity. The byway parallels the Carson River and the Pony Express Trail, climbs the lonely Pine Nut Mountains, and crosses barren desert and irrigated cropland.

The route consists of thirty-eight miles of gravel Type I road and twenty-nine miles of rough Type II road. The gravel sections are mostly two-lane

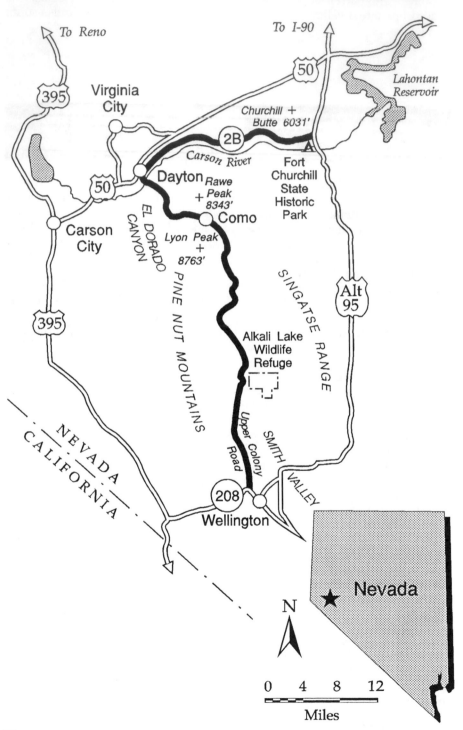

To Reno

To I-90

395

Virginia City

50

Lahontan Reservoir

Churchill + Butte 6031'

2B

Carson River

Fort Churchill State Historic Park

50

Dayton

Rawe Peak 8343'

EL DORADO CANYON

Como

Carson City

Lyon Peak 8763'

SINGATSE RANGE

Alt 95

PINE NUT MOUNTAINS

Alkali Lake Wildlife Refuge

395

Upper Colony Road

SMITH VALLEY

NEVADA

CALIFORNIA

208

Wellington

Nevada

N

0   4   8   12
Miles

and passable year-round. The rough segment over the Pine Nut Mountains features a single-lane road with steep grades and pullouts for passing and views. It is very rocky in places and impassable in winter. A high-clearance, two-wheel drive vehicle is necessary to safely drive the entire byway. A four-wheel drive is recommended during wet weather. The byway requires four to five hours to drive.

Summer and fall are the best seasons to drive the byway. The route climbs 3,000 feet from the Carson River over the Pine Nut Mountains. Expect daily high temperatures to range from fifty to over ninety degrees. Nights can be chilly. Summer thunderstorms are common in the mountains. Spring is generally cool and windy, while winters are cold.

The byway begins by turning west on Nevada Highway 2B at Fort Churchill State Historic Monument thirty-five miles east of Carson City via U.S. 50 and Alternate U.S. 95 or twenty-four miles south of Fernley and Interstate 80 on Alternate U.S. 95.

Fort Churchill, part of the Nevada State Park system since 1957, was established in 1860 to protect the Pony Express mail line and neighboring settlers from maurading Paiutes and Bannocks. The fort, named for Inspector General of the Army Sylvester Churchill, consisted of fifty-eight buildings, including barracks, officer's quarters, offices, storerooms, barns, a hospital, an arsenal, and a jail. The Civil War heightened Fort Churchill's importance by helping to insure Nevada's loyalty to the Union and serving as a supply depot for the Nevada Military District. The post was abandoned in 1869 and sold at auction for $750. Today the fort has a visitor center with historic exhibits, a picnic area, and a spacious twenty-unit campground shaded by towering cottonwood trees along the Carson River.

The byway heads west along the tree-lined Carson River from Fort Churchill on a gravel, washboarded road. The river makes lazy bends past ranches, alfalfa fields, and grazing horses and cattle through its wide valley. Dry, sagebrush-covered hills surround the valley. At one place, Table Mountain juts its thick brow of vertical basalt cliffs over the road. The high, forested ridges of the Pine Nut Mountains rise south of here, lifting up to the rounded 8,343-foot summit of Rawe Peak.

The road, as it follows the river, also parallels the old route of the historic Pony Express Trail. The 1,800-mile trail from St. Joseph, Missouri to Sacramento, California operated eighteen months between April 3, 1860 and October 28, 1861. The cost per half-ounce letter was $5 and took ten days for delivery. After the completion of the first transcontinental telegraph line, the Pony Express went out of business.

The Pony Express Trail roughly followed today's U.S. 50 across Nevada. It dipped south to Fort Churchill and headed west to Carson City and the Sierra Nevada. One of the most famous riders on this trail segment was "Pony Bob" Haslam. His regular route ran from Buckland's Station near Fort Churchill to Lake Tahoe. He once rode the 120 miles in eight hours and twenty minutes, while wounded by Indians and carrying President Lincoln's Inaugural Address.

After twenty-one miles the byway reaches the historic town of Dayton, twelve miles east of Carson City, at the junction of Gold Creek and the Carson River. This area was once used by Washoe Indians for river fishing, pinenut gathering, and as a winter campground. Dayton was the site of Nevada's first gold strike. Fabulous silver lodes, later discovered on the Comstock, led to a silver rush. First settled in 1849, the town was named for town surveyor

Fort Churchill, a Nevada State Monument on the Fort Churchill to Wellington Byway, was built along the Pony Express Trail in 1860.

John Day in 1861. That same year the Rock Point Mill was built to crush ore from the famed Comstock mines. The town population grew to 2,500 by 1865. The mill operated sporadically until the 1920s.

Dayton is now a reminder of Nevada's boom and bust mining days. Parts of the old mill can be seen at Dayton State Park. The park has a ten-site campground, picnic area, and historic displays. Dayton has complete services for the traveler, including motels, restaurants, and service stations.

The byway crosses the Carson River in Dayton, passes the local high school, and turns south on the BLM's Como Road toward the Pine Nut Mountains. The road crosses a broad, sagebrush-covered outwash plain before climbing steeply into the mountains above Eldorado Canyon. As the byway gains elevation, the road enters into a pinyon pine and juniper forest.

After a few miles, the byway turns east and passes abandoned mines and tailings in the Como Mining District. Shortly afterward the road crosses a wide saddle between Rawe Peak to the north and 8,763-foot Lyon Peak to the south. There are four-wheel drive trails north of here. The area is also a popular spot for collecting pinyon pinenuts. Up to twenty-five pounds can be collected without a permit.

Past the saddle, the road narrows to single-lane and bumps south down a winding canyon to a wide sagebrush meadow. The byway, continuing south, becomes rough and cobbled. Past the meadow it dips sharply into a rock-rimmed canyon and winds down the rocky wash. This byway segment is remote and unpeopled. Wildlife abounds, including mule deer, bobcats, mountain lions, coyotes, and wild horses. Hawks, eagles, and vultures ride the winds overhead.

Further down, the canyon widens and becomes a valley, flanked on the west by the wall of the Pine Nut Mountains and on the east by the low barren Buckskin Range. The byway, providing access to ranches in Churchill Canyon, follows the graded, gravel Sunrise Pass Road. After about seven miles, the byway drops into broad Smith Valley.

Alkali Lake sits at the valley's north end. The lake, a dry, white pan in summer, is managed for waterfowl as the Alkali Lake Wildlife Management Area. South of the lake, the byway bumps up against the steep Pine Nut Mountains then heads into Smith Valley past pastoral farms green with irrigated crops. The last few miles of the byway is on paved Upper Colony Road and ends at Wellington on Nevada Highway 208. A right turn leads to U.S. 395, Carson City, and Yosemite National Park. A left turn goes through Wellington, and on to U.S. 95, Fort Churchill, and Interstate 80.

19 WILD RIVERS
New Mexico

General description: A Type I, thirteen-mile-long, paved road that parallels the deep gorges of the Rio Grande and Red River in northern New Mexico.
Special attractions: Camping, backpacking, fishing, hiking, photography, wildlife observation, birdwatching, bicycling, scenic views, visitor center, interpretative programs, Rio Grande Wild and Scenic River.
Location: Northern New Mexico near Questa, twenty-six miles north of Taos and seventeen miles south of the Colorado and New Mexico state line. Reach the byway by turning west on New Mexico Highway 378 from New Mexico Highway 3 about two miles north of Questa. Highway 522 turns into the byway when it reaches the border of the BLM Wild Rivers Recreation Area.
Byway route name: Wild Rivers Road.
Travel season: Year-round. The byway is unmaintained during the winter when snow can close access.
Camping: Twenty-one campsites in five campgrounds in Wild Rivers Recreation Area and fifteen developed backpacker campsites in the river canyons. Primitive camping is allowed at the top of the Guadalupe Trail. No hook-ups. A fee is charged at the developed rim campgrounds. Campfires are allowed in grills only.
Services: All services are available in Questa and Taos.
Nearby attractions: Taos, Taos Pueblo, Ski Rio Ski Area, Rio Grande Gorge, Red River Fish Hatchery, Governor Bent Home and Museum, Kit Carson Home and Museum, Fort Burgwin Research Center, Carson National Forest, Eagle Nest Lake, Uracca State Wildlife Area, Red River Ski Area, Taos Ski Valley, Angel Fire Ski Area.
For more information: BLM, Taos Resource Area, Monte Vista Plaza, 224 Cruz Alta Road, Taos, NM 87571. (505) 758-8851.

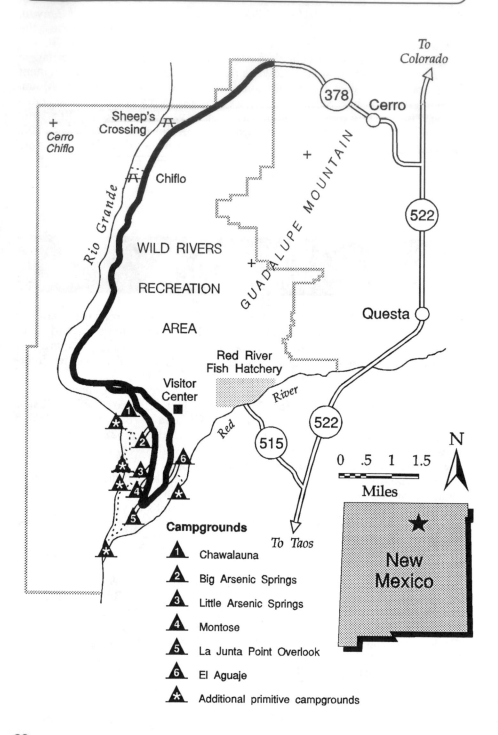

To
Colorado

378

Cerro

Sheep's
Crossing

+
Cerro
Chiflo

Chiflo

Rio Grande

WILD RIVERS

RECREATION

AREA

GUADALUPE MOUNTAIN

522

Questa

Red River
Fish Hatchery

Visitor
Center

Red   River

515

522

0   .5   1   1.5

Miles

N

1

2

6

3

4

5

Campgrounds

To Taos

1 Chawalauna

2 Big Arsenic Springs

3 Little Arsenic Springs

4 Montose

5 La Junta Point Overlook

6 El Aguaje

★ Additional primitive campgrounds

New
Mexico

The trip: The Wild Rivers Back Country Byway parallels a spectacular stretch of the Rio Grande as it winds through a gorge that reaches 800 feet deep at its confluence with the Red River. The byway offers scenic views of the towering peaks of the Sangre de Cristo Range, a hike up an ancient volcano, fishing in the river's deep pools, views of some of North America's most difficult rapids, backpacking into the gorge's wild depths, camping on the canyon rim, and twelve miles of developed trails. The paved, two-lane byway has numerous pullouts and scenic overlooks. Allow one to two hours to drive the byway; longer if you want to hike down to the canyon bottom.

Summer visitors can expect pleasantly warm temperatures with daily highs between sixty-five and ninety degrees. Nights are cool. Heavy thunderstorms typically occur on July and August afternoons. Autumns are cooler and dry, with highs in the sixties and seventies. Winters are cold, with snow on the ground. The road is unmaintained and snowfall often closes the road completely. Spring is cool and often windy.

The byway is accessed from New Mexico Highway 522, two miles north of Questa and seventeen miles south of the Colorado and New Mexico state line. Turn west on New Mexico Highway 378 and pass through Cerro, an old farming community founded in 1854. The road bends west past the forested north slope of Guadalupe Mountain and after about three miles reaches the border of the BLM's Wild Rivers Recreation Area and the start of the byway. The road traverses another mile across the wide sagebrush and grass-covered plain of the Taos Plateau before reaching the abrupt river gorge at Sheep's Crossing.

This first glimpse of the Rio Grande is spectacular. The river tumbles over water-worn boulders far below the basalt-rimmed overlook. Upstream lies the rounded hump of 10,093-foot Ute Mountain, a shield volcano formed of fine-grained dacite. Gnarled, weathered junipers dot the canyon slopes and brilliant lichens cover rough boulders along the rim. Sheep's Crossing also has two picnic sites and pit toilets.

The Rio Grande, for forty-eight miles from the Colorado border south to the Taos Junction Bridge, was designated in 1968, along with the last four miles of the Red River, as one of the nation's first Wild and Scenic Rivers. The Bureau of Land Management preserves and protects the wilderness character of the rivers for future Americans to enjoy. The Rio Grande, America's second longest river, begins on the Continental Divide in Colorado's San Juan Mountains and ends 1,885 miles later in the Gulf of Mexico.

Here, on the Wild Rivers byway, the river slices down through the Taos Plateau leaving one of the Southwest's most beautiful and remote canyons. The river follows the Rio Grande Rift, a long, narrow region between El Paso, Texas and Alamosa, Colorado where the earth's crust is slowly pulling apart along faults. As the crust separates, the center of the rift drops to form a valley and the sides rise to form mountains. The rift at the Taos Plateau is filled with alternate layers of gravel and sediment washed from the eroding Sangre de Cristo Range and thick layers of black basalt from now-extinct volcanos. The canyon itself did not form by the rift action, but was carved by river erosion over the last two million years.

From Sheep's Crossing the byway travels almost a mile along the rim to Chiflo Overlook. Here is a great view across the river to 8,976-foot Cerro Chiflo, an ancient volcano covered with a thick pinyon pine and juniper forest. The wind whistles over this round-shouldered mountain giving it the Spanish name which means "whistle hill." The popular Chiflo Trail drops a quarter mile down to the river from the overlook. Nearby are three shaded picnic tables and restrooms.

A mile south of Chiflo, a left turn leads to the Guadalupe Mountain trailhead. This trail climbs through a pinyon pine and juniper woodland to the extinct volcano's 8,722-foot summit. The 360 degree panaroma includes views of the snowcapped Sangre de Cristos and the river gorges below.

Excellent views of the Rio Grande are seen at Bear Crossing. The canyon walls stairstep down from the rim to the river, with thick basalt layers forming cliffs and pale gravel rubble sloping between them.

From Bear Crossing the byway crosses a fault line and rises into a pinyon pine and juniper woodland, with scattered ponderosa pines growing on moister

The Rio Grande carves an impressive canyon alongside the Wild Rivers Byway.

slopes. A couple miles along the canyon rim leads to a road junction. Here the byway forms an open loop. It's best to turn east here. The Arthur W. Zimmerman Visitor Center lies just down the byway. The center, open Memorial Day through Labor Day, offers interpretive displays and handouts on the area's geology, natural history, cultural resources, and recreational opportunities. There are also nature hikes and programs.

The byway heads south from the visitor center and passes several popular recreation sites along the canyon rim. First is El Aguaje. Here lie five campsites along the rim of the Red River and the trailhead for .75 mile El Aguaje Trail. This trail falls steeply down to the Red River, renowned for its excellent rainbow and German brown trout fishing.

La Junta Point, 880 feet above the confluence of the Red River and the Rio Grande, has six picnic/campsites, a short self-guided nature trail, and the one-mile La Junta Trail to the canyon bottom. The Rio Grande has a very steep gradient here, dropping 650 feet in the twelve miles above the Red River junction. This gradient, coupled with immense boulders sheared off the canyon walls, creates a series of foaming, unnavigable rapids rated Class VI by boaters. Rafters float the more managable water in the Upper Taos Box above Chiflo and the Lower Taos Box below La Junta Point.

Just north of La Junta lie Montoso, Little Arsenic Springs, and Big Arsenic Springs overlooks and campgrounds. The three areas have eleven campsites, water, and restrooms. Two popular one-mile-long paths, Little Arsenic Springs Trail and Big Arsenic Springs Trail, wend down from the overlooks to the river. Established backpacker campsites are along the river.

Hikers need to wear sturdy shoes, carry rain gear and first aid supplies, and lots of water. Swimming in the river is not recommended, there are dangerous currents. Keep an eye out for poison ivy and rattlesnakes. Permits are not required for backpacking in the canyon; they are needed, however, for all river runners.

Chawaluana Overlook is the last stop before the byway loop ends. A short walk leads from the parking area to Chawalauna or "hole-in-the-rock." Here a section of basalt cliff has broken away from the rim and a small window has eroded through it. There are dramatic views of the gorge below and the low volcanos west of the byway. It's also a good place to sit on the rim, watch cloud shadows trail across the rugged terrain, and remember the value of a river's untamed spirit.

General description: A twenty-four-mile, Type II byway that traverses a wild desert landscape of canyons, escarpments, and ridges east of the Rio Grande in central New Mexico.

Special attractions: Rio Grande, desert wildlife, Tinajas Area of Critical Environmental Concern, Presilla Wilderness Study Area, Sierra de las Canas Wilderness Study Area, hiking, backpacking, primitive camping.

Location: Central New Mexico east of Socorro. The byway's northern access is at the Escondida Exit, #152, on Interstate 25 two miles north of Socorro. Drive 1.5 miles north of Escondida and take a right turn past Escondida Lake to Pueblitos. Turn south and after .6 mile make a sharp left turn onto the byway. Southern access is on U.S. Highway 380 about eleven miles east of San Antonio and Interstate 25. Turn north on County Road A-129. The byway starts three miles north.

Byway route name: Quebradas Road.

Travel season: Year-round. Heavy rain can make several dry wash crossings impassable.

Camping: Primitive camping along the entire byway. Bring water.

Services: All services are available in Socorro and San Antonio.

Nearby attractions: Socorro, Mineralogical Museum (N.M. Institute of Mining and Technology), Bosque del Apache National Wildlife Refuge, Sevilleta National Wildlife Refuge, La Joya State Wildlife Area, San Pasqual Wilderness Area, Withington Wilderness Area, Apache Kid Wilderness Area, Cibola National Forest.

For more information: BLM, Socorro Resource Area Office, 198 Neel Avenue N.W., Socorro, NM 87801. (505) 835-0412.

The trip: The Quebradas Back Country Byway traverses remote Chihuahuan Desert country east of Socorro in central New Mexico. The Type II byway is bordered on the east by the rugged, barren Lomas de las Canas uplift, a highland between the Rio Grande Valley to the west and the Jornada del Muerto Basin to the east. The dirt road follows wide arroyos, crosses rocky ridges, dips into steep canyons, and offers outstanding views of the towering mountain ranges west of Socorro. The byway requires high-clearance vehicles because of several rocky wash crossings and sandy sections. The road becomes very slippery in wet weather. The byway takes two to three hours to drive.

Weather along the byway is generally moderate year-round. Summers can be hot with maximum temperatures of ninety to 100 degrees. Winters are mild, with daily highs in the forties. Spring and fall are ideal times to drive the byway, although spring is typically windy. Rainfall averages ten inches a year, with over half coming between July and September. Intense thunderstorms cause flash floods, so care must be taken during inclement weather.

Begin by exiting Interstate 25 at the Escondida Exit, #152, two miles north of Socorro. The road, after leaving Escondida, turns north and after 1.5 miles reaches a sharp right turn that passes Escondida Lake, crosses the shallow,

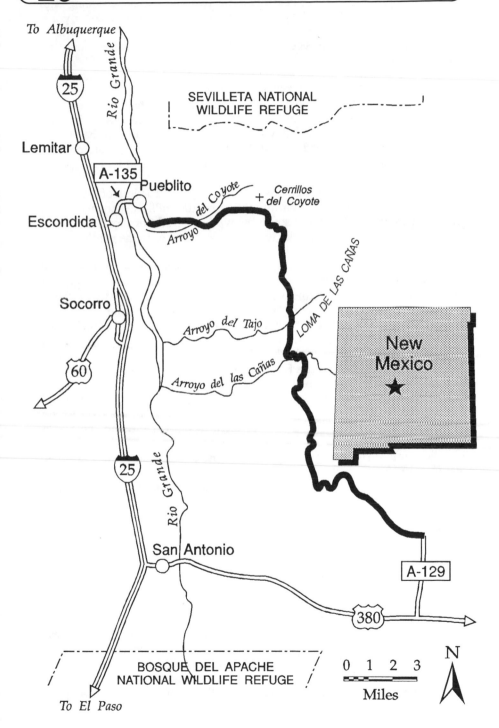

To Albuquerque

Rio Grande

25

SEVILLETA NATIONAL
WILDLIFE REFUGE

Lemitar

A-135

Pueblito

Arroyo del Coyote

+ Cerrillos
del Coyote

Escondida

LOMA DE LAS CAÑAS

Socorro

Arroyo del Tajo

New
Mexico
★

60

Arroyo del las Cañas

25

Rio Grande

San Antonio

A-129

380

N

0 1 2 3
Miles

BOSQUE DEL APACHE
NATIONAL WILDLIFE REFUGE

To El Paso

tamarisk-lined Rio Grande, and enters the small village of Pueblitos. On the south side of town the road becomes gravel. After six-tenths of a mile look for Quebradas Back Country Byway, a narrow dirt road that turns sharply east.

The road follows broad Arroyo del Coyote for two miles before climbing onto a barren ridge. This sere landscape, broken by dry washes, box-canyons, limestone ridges, and sandstone hills, represents one of New Mexico's least disturbed Chihuahuan Desert ecosystems. The scrubby vegetation along the byway is typical of the upper Chihuahuan Desert.

Creosote, the dominant plant, sparsely covers the desert floor, thriving where little else will grow. Each plant stakes its own water rights by sucking up moisture around itself. This stingy bush with yellow blossoms has small leathery leaves to impede evaporation. Other common plants along the byway include black grama grass, cholla cactus, datil yucca, prickly pear cactus, Apache plume, ocotillo, squawbush, snakeweed, and Mormon tea. Along the dry watercourses grow twisted honey mesquite, and in places, pygmy forests of widely spaced juniper.

The road continues over low mesas, rimmed by tilted layers of limestone deposited in a shallow marine environment some 200 million years ago. After five miles the byway makes a turn south below the ragged Cerrillos del Coyote. This is a good place to park and hike up a dry wash and onto the gentle mountain ridges.

The byway, heading south, borders the faulted western edge of the Loma de las Canas uplift. These mountains, hills, and mesas form a low highland between the Rio Grande Rift to the west and the wide Jornada del Muerto Basin to the east. This range is composed of stacked layers of sandstone, shale, and limestone. It is also the 12,838-acre Sierra de las Canas Wilderness Study Area. The 8,680-acre Presilla Wilderness Study Area lies west of the byway. Both areas offer great opportunities for backpacking, hiking, solitude, and exploration.

After turning south, Quebradas Road follows a side-canyon of Arroyo de los Pinos to a low divide. The canyon, rimmed on the west by a cap of erosion-resistant limestone, is a good place to spot hawks, eagles, and vultures perched on the rimrock. A short cross-country hike climbs west from the road to the ridge and offers marvelous views of the Cerrillos del Coyote and the Sierra de las Canas.

The wilderness surrounding the byway is home to over 200 wildlife species. Big game animals are mule deer and pronghorn. Predators include coyotes, bobcats, gray foxes, and badgers. Other mammals are desert cottontails, jackrabbits, mice, and squirrels. Birds seen are golden eagles, red-tailed hawks, sparrowhawks, horned larks, pinyon jays, and ravens. Reptiles encountered include western diamond-backed rattlesnakes, bull snakes, collared lizards, and fence lizards.

The byway, heading south, traverses between low, swelling ridges dotted with juniper and creosote, and dips into the shallow washes of Arroyo Tinajas and Arroyo del Tajo. A great hike follows Arroyo del Tajo west through a sharp V-shaped portal of limestone cliffs and into the Presilla Wilderness Study Area.

After leaving Arroyo del Tajo, the byway follows a broad ridge before dropping steeply into Arroyo de las Canas. The sierra sweeps up east of the road above a sandy, tamarisk-lined wash that drains a deep canyon carved into the escarpment's face. The road climbs out of the arroyo and crosses a wide benchland seamed with shallow canyons for five miles.

The byway turns east at the southern end of the Loma de Las Canas up an

The Quebradas Byway traverses a juniper-studded valley beneath the Sierra de las Canas.

arroyo that enters a wide valley surrounded by barren, rolling mountains. The road skirts the valley's southern edge before climbing over a low divide and passing onto the western perimeter of the Jornada del Muerto Basin.

Great views unfold from the divide. West towers the rugged Magdalena Mountains above Socorro. East lies the mostly flat, dry intermountain basin called the Jornada del Muerto, or "journey of the dead one." Early Spanish travelers between El Paso and Santa Fe left the Rio Grande River north of Las Cruces and journeyed ninety miles up the arid basin. Today, most of the plain is part of the White Sands Missile Range. The world's first A-bomb was exploded here at Trinity Site on July 16, 1945.

The byway leaves the low mountains behind and rolls across the edge of the broad valley. It dips into sandy Canon Agua Buena, before ending on Socorro County Road A-129. A right turn on the unpaved road leads three miles to U.S. 280, a major highway connecting San Antonio and Carrizozo. San Antonio and Interstate 25 are eleven miles west on the highway.

Byway travelers will want to visit the Bosque del Apache National Wildlife Refuge south of San Antonio. The preserve, established in 1939, protects important winter habitat for sandhill and whooping cranes. October through January are the best times to view the birds. Other birds seen here include great blue herons, sandhill cranes, eagles, and a variety of ducks and geese. A self-guiding auto tour threads through the refuge.

21 LAKEVIEW to STEENS
Oregon

General description: A ninety-mile, Type I and II byway that crosses a wide variety of landscapes and ecosystems between Lakeview and Frenchglen in south-central Oregon.

Special attractions: Fremont National Forest, Hart Mountain National Antelope Refuge, Warner Valley wetlands, camping, hiking, wildlife watching and photography, hot springs, rockhounding.

Location: South-central Oregon. The byway leaves U.S. 395 five miles north of Lakeview or twenty miles north of the California border and travels east on Oregon Highway 140 for sixteen miles. Byway turns north here and follows paved Lake County Road 3-13 to Plush. Past Plush a gravel road leads up through Hart Mountain National Antelope Refuge and across the Catlow Valley to Oregon Highway 206 seven miles south of Frenchglen.

Byway route numbers: Oregon Highway 140, Lake County Road 3-13.

Travel season: Byway is open year-round, although snow can close the road temporarily until it is plowed.

Camping: Deep Creek and Mud Creek campgrounds in Fremont National Forest off Oregon Highway 140. Goose Lake State Park, fifteen miles south of Lakeview on U.S. 395, has forty-eight campsites, showers, and water. At Hart Mountain National Antelope Refuge is Hot Springs Camp, a primitive campground three miles south of refuge headquarters. Primitive camping is allowed on BLM lands along the byway.

Services: All services at Lakeview. Limited services, including gas and groceries, at Plush and Frenchglen.

Nearby attractions: Steens Mountain Back Country Byway, Barrel Springs Back Country Byway, Malheur National Wildlife Refuge, Frenchglen Hotel State Wayside Park, Goose Lake State Park.

For more information: BLM, Lakeview District Office, 1000 Ninth Street S., P.O. Box 151, Lakeview, OR 97630. (503) 947-2177.

The trip: The Lakeview to Steens Back Country Byway travels ninety miles across Oregon's high Great Basin Desert through a variety of ecosystems from Sonoran to Hudsonian, past great shallow lakes and wetlands in Warner Valley, and over Hart Mountain, a dramatic fault-block mountain. This is a land of wild views—distant snowcapped mountains that hover, like clouds, over far

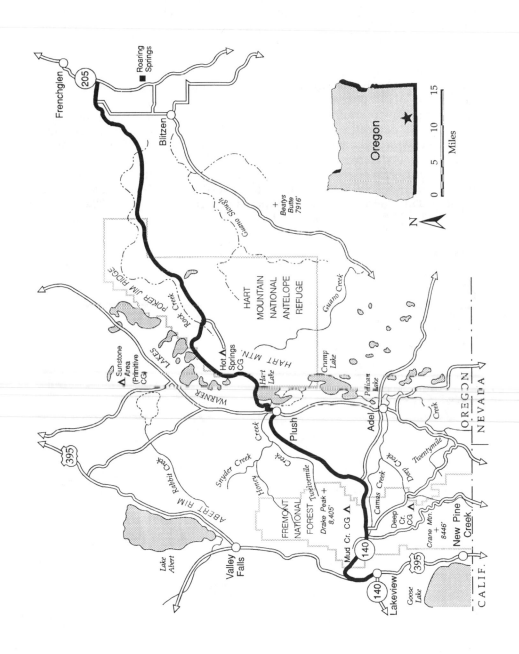

horizons; mirages that shimmer over immense dry lakebeds; and sagebrush that spreads a grey carpet across low hills broken by intermittent canyons and rimrock lava flows.

Traffic along the byway's forty paved miles and fifty gravel miles is sporadic. The road is mostly two-lane, with one section just east of Hart Mountain National Antelope Refuge being one-and-a-half-lanes and lightly maintained. The byway is driven easily in a passenger car, although a four-wheel drive is needed to explore backroads on the refuge. Make sure to top off your gas tank before embarking on the byway, particularly if you plan on traveling side roads along the way. Don't plan on gas at either Plush or Frenchglen during any other time than regular business hours. Allow three or four hours to drive the byway.

The byway is open year-round. Winter snow and mud can, however, close the road or create adverse driving conditions. Summer and autumn are the best times to explore the Lakeview to Steens Byway. Temperatures range from seventy to 100 degrees, with nights, especially atop Hart Mountain, considerably cooler. Most of the annual precipitation in this high desert falls in summer thunderstorms, otherwise the days are generally clear and sunny.

The byway begins five miles north of Lakeview at the junction of U.S. 395 and Oregon 140. Lakeview, situated at the north end of Goose Lake Valley, was settled in 1889 as a livestock, timber, and agricultural center. The town's economy is still based on this trio. Lakeview, in an active geothermal area,

Drake Peak rises beyond the Lakeview to Steens Byway.

has Oregon's only continuous geyser, "Old Perpetual", at Hunter's Hot Springs on the town's north edge. It erupts about twice a minute. Goose Lake spreads across the valley south of Lakeview. An Oregon State Park on the lake's east shore has forty-eight campsites with hookups and showers.

From the junction of U.S. 395 and Oregon 140, the byway heads eastward into the Warner Mountains and quickly climbs up through a ponderosa pine and Douglas fir forest to 5,846-foot-high Warner Pass. Warner Canyon Ski Area, at the pass summit, offers downhill and cross-country skiing. This section of the byway crosses Fremont National Forest. Two campgrounds, Mud Creek and Deep Creek, are north and south respectively of the byway. Other forest recreation includes hiking the Crane Mountain National Recreation Trail and excellent fishing at Overton Reservoir and Vee Lake.

The road drops from the pass into a broad grassy valley, before entering a small canyon carved by Camas Creek. Be alert for a left turn onto Lake County Road 3-13. The two-lane, paved road traverses northward below 8,405-foot Drake Peak. The historic Fort Bidwell to Fort Warner Road, an old military trail, crosses Drake Peak west of the byway and heads north to the site of old Fort Warner on Honey Creek. The byway, after nineteen miles, reaches Plush in Warner Valley.

Plush, an old ranching center, boasted a population of 2,000 back in the 1920s. Now it's a quiet, shady stop along the byway with a few homes and an all-purpose general store and service station. Legend says the town got its name in a poker game. One local with a speech impediment, laid his cards down on the table and announced excitedly he had a "plush." The name stuck.

The byway meanders north from Plush across the lush Warner Valley. The valley, a long basin in the morning shadow of Hart Mountain, is filled with landlocked swamplands and a chain of shallow, interconnected lakes. In spring and early summer the lakes brim with melted runoff, their waters edged with grass and reeds, and filled with rafts of birds, including snow geese, pelicans, egrets, cranes, and ducks. Much of the private ranchland between Plush and Hart Lake supports marshes, birds, hay fields, and cattle.

North of Hart Lake lies the Warner Wetlands Area of Critical Environmental Concern, a fifteen-mile swath of BLM land dedicated to wetland habitat preservation. The BLM, while allowing multiple use, is slowly restoring these lakes and swamps to their aboriginal richness. Planned developments include campgrounds, hiking trails, and handicap access. The Oregon state gemstone, the Sunstone, is also found in northern Warner Valley. The BLM set aside a special collecting area north of the lakes for amateur collectors. A map and information is available at the Lakeview BLM office.

The byway enters 275,000-acre Hart Mountain National Antelope Refuge just past Hart Lake. The refuge, established in 1936 to protect dwindling antelope herds, provides important habitat for not only antelope but over 300 wildlife species, including mule deer, bighorn sheep, and many large birds of prey. The pronghorn antelope, an amazingly fleet mammal, has been clocked at speeds of forty miles an hour. They are often seen along the byway near refuge headquarters and in the sagebrush as the byway drops toward the refuge's eastern boundary.

In the refuge, the road parallels the towering, west-facing, basalt escarpment of Hart Mountain and Poker Jim Ridge. This fault-block mountain rises precipitously from Warner Valley, lifting 3,600-feet from the valley floor to the 8,065-foot summit of Warner Peak. The byway climbs the rugged face,

A burrowing owl on the Hart Mountain National Antelope Refuge along the Lakeview to Steens Byway.

passing deep gorges and steep cliffs. Marvelous views unfold from the byway as it ascends.

The refuge headquarters and a small museum lie a few miles beyond the mountain rim. Hot Springs Camp, a primitive campground with a hot springs bathhouse, nestles in a valley three miles south of headquarters. Wildlife watching and photography is the refuge's most popular activity.

The byway continues down Hart Mountain's east side over a gently sloping series of hills, ridges, and plains that forms the west edge of broad Catlow Valley. As glaciers retreated during the Pleistocene Epoch some 10,000 years ago, the valley was a vast, seventy-foot-deep lake. Wide vistas unfold from the byway as it crosses the refuge's eastern boundary. Snowcapped 9,733-foot Steens Mountain lies almost fifty miles eastward, while to the south rises conical 7,885-foot Beaty Butte.

Several historic ranches and abandoned homesteads dating from the 1880s dot the sagebrush-covered valley. Ragtown, Beckley, and Blitzen were three towns that once served the homesteaders, but most along with their dreams for this high desert land vanished by 1920. Today, the valley's few fertile acres are devoted to hay and livestock grazing. The byway, after crossing almost thirty miles of the wide desolate valley, ends at paved Oregon Highway 206. Seven miles north is historic Frenchglen, Malheur National Wildlife Refuge, and the beginning of the Steens Mountain Byway.

General description: A Type I and II, 102-mile route through central Oregon, past recent lava flows and cinder cones, sand dunes, a "lost forest," and historic sites.

Special attractions: Fort Rock State Park, Devils Garden Wilderness Study Area, Squaw Ridge Wilderness Study Area, Four Craters Wilderness Study Area, Crack-in-the-Ground, Fossil Lake, Sand Dunes Wilderness Study Area, Lost Forest Research Natural Area, Derrick Cave, hiking, rockhounding, and camping.

Location: Central Oregon, about seventy miles east of Crater Lake National Park. The open loop begins at the Fort Rock turnoff on Oregon Highway 31, eighteen miles north of Silver Lake and thirty-five miles southeast of LaPine. The byway follows a series of paved and unpaved county and BLM roads, some requiring four-wheel drive or high-clearance vehicles. There are, however, byway segments that bypass the rough gravel roads, allowing the entire byway to be driven in a passenger car.

Byway route numbers: Lake County Roads 5-10, 5-12, 5-12B, 5-14C, 5-14D, 5-14E, 5-14F, and BLM Road 6109.

Travel season: The byway is open year-round. Some segments, however, will be closed in winter by snow, including the road over Green Mountain and the road to the Sand Dunes and Lost Forest. These roads are also subject to flooding and extremely muddy conditions from March through May.

Camping: Primitive camping is allowed on BLM land along the byway. Look for already established sites. One of the best places is among the pines at Lost Forest. A primitive BLM campground, without water or sanitary facilities, is located just below the summit of Green Mountain. There are also campgrounds in Fremont National Forest south of Silver Lake.

Services: All services are available at Silver Lake and Christmas Valley. Limited services are at Fort Rock.

Nearby attractions: Lower Crooked River Back Country Byway, Lakeview to Steens Back Country Byway, Crater Lake National Park, Klamath Forest National Wildlife Refuge, Newberry Crater, Summer Lake Hot Springs, LaPine Recreation Area, and Gearhart Mountain Wilderness Area.

For more information: BLM, Lakeview District Office, 1000 Ninth Street South, P.O. Box 151, Lakeview, OR 97630. (503) 947-2177. Maps and brochures are available.

The trip: Set among the bold volcanic features of central Oregon, the Christmas Valley Back Country Byway traverses 102 miles of paved and unpaved roads east of Oregon Highway 31. It crosses a harsh, austere land of sagebrush, lava flows, cinder cones, and sand dunes, but it also passes green alfalfa fields, paddocks of fat cattle, and a golf course.

The byway, with twelve miles of rough roads, requires a high-clearance vehicle to drive its entire length. Alternate routes, however, bypass the rough segments and allow the route to be driven in a passenger car. The byway is a combination of double-lane paved and gravel roads, and single-lane dirt roads

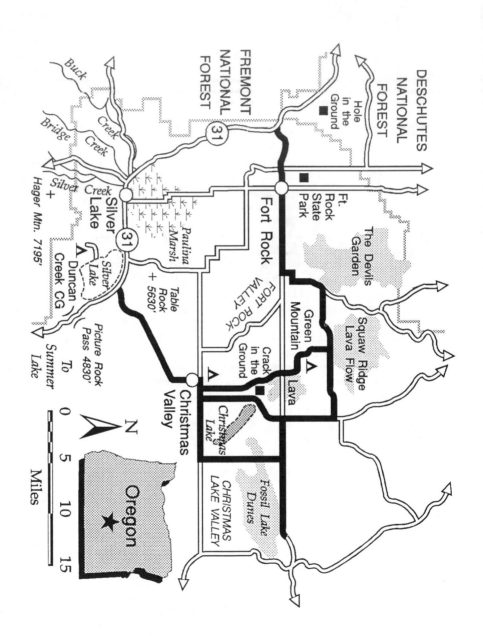

with turnouts. Allow at least six hours to drive the complete byway route.

The byway is open year-round, although snow and mud close sections of the road during winter and spring. Summer and fall are pleasant in this high desert. Daily temperatures are usually between eighty and 100 degrees. Nights are much cooler, dropping down to fifty. It is advisable, as on most back country byways, to carry sufficient water and supplies in case of breakdown.

Christmas Valley Byway leaves Oregon Highway 31 at the Fort Rock turn, eighteen miles north of Silver Lake, in a region of low hills spotted with ponderosa pine. The road travels east through a flattening valley for six miles to the small community of Fort Rock. The Homestead Village Museum, on the town's west edge, preserves the area's homestead era with an early church, two typical homestead homes, a log cabin, and a pioneer doctor's office.

Fort Rock, the town's namesake, sits one mile north of the byway. The red walls of this immense stone stockade, a Registered Natural Landmark, tower 300 feet above the flat plain. The rock is one third of a mile in diameter. Geologists call Fort Rock a volcanic tuff ring or maar. It formed between 10,000 and 20,000 years ago when today's Fort Rock Valley was part of an ancient lake that covered as much as 200 square miles and was 200 feet deep. Molten lava, rising from deep in the earth's core, met water-saturated rocks beneath the lake's surface. The resulting steam produced violent explosions and hurled hot ash and rock fragments high in the air like a huge fountain. The ash and rock fell in a circle around the volcanic vent and solidified into the tuff ring. It may have formed in only a few days or months. Waves, driven by winds, eroded away the south part of the ring and gave the rock its horseshoe shape. Fort Rock State Park, a 160-acre area, offers trails, shaded picnic tables, and modern restrooms.

Cow Cave, two miles west of Fort Rock in Beggarheel Butte, was the site of one of North America's most astonishing archeological finds in 1938. Dr. Luther Cressman from the University of Oregon uncovered seventy-five Indian sandals woven from twisted sagebrush bark over 9,000 years old, along with basketry, scrapers, knives, awls, and animal bones. These mark Cow Cave as one of North America's oldest known human habitation sites.

From Fort Rock, the byway continues east for eight miles on paved Lake County Road 5-12 before turning north on a bladed gravel road into a scrubby juniper forest. Old fencelines and weatherworn buildings mark the sites of abandoned homesteads along the roadside. Turn-of-the-century homesteaders relied on fickle rainfall to grow crops in this dry valley, and when the rains failed, their dreams, fortunes, and plants withered away. In 1938, the Bankhead-Jones Act returned the abandoned farms to Federal ownership.

After the byway turns away from Fort Rock Valley, it passes Devils Garden Lava Bed Wilderness Study Area and Squaw Ridge Lava Bed Wilderness Study Area. Both are remote, unspoiled, and very rugged. Devils Garden, composed of smooth pahoehoe lava, offers opportunities for hiking and backpacking. It is also an outdoor classroom for geology students. Squaw Ridge, on the north edge of the byway, is a large lava flow with several cinder cones. It is made up of aa lava, a rough, sharp rock that is extremely difficult to hike across.

If you turn north at Devils Garden and drive eight miles, a short spur road leads to Derrick Cave. This unique lava tube cave is over a quarter-of-a-mile long and reaches heights of thirty feet. In the early 1960s, it was stocked with provisions and water for use as a fallout shelter.

Directly opposite Squaw Ridge lava flow, the byway turns south on BLM

A hiker in the unique Crack-in-the-Ground along the Christmas Valley Byway.

Road 6109 C toward Green Mountain. This road section is steep and rough. Passenger cars are advised to take an alternate route by continuing east on County Road 5-12B for seven miles to County Road 5-14C. Turn south and drive six miles to the road to the Lost Forest.

The byway climbs up through a thick juniper forest to the summit of 5,190-foot Green Mountain. A two-story fire lookout sits atop the mountain. Visitors are welcome, unless fire operations are in progress. The view is simply spectacular, with all of Christmas and Fort Rock valleys spread out below. Snowcapped Diamond Peak in the Cascades lies seventy miles to the west, while Wagontire Mountain bulges fifty miles eastward. Just south of the mountain summit is a five-site, primitive BLM campground. It has no sanitary facilities or water.

Dropping off Green Mountain, the byway borders Four Craters Lava Bed Wilderness Study Area. Along the road are four cinder cones, between 250 and 400 feet high, that give the area its name. Blocky lava flows that came from the craters push up along the edge of the byway. Junipers, grass, and sagebrush have begun to colonize this jagged, inhospitable environment.

Crack-in-the-Ground, another of the byway's distinctive volcanic features, lies just east of the road near the wilderness study area boundary. Crack-in-the-Ground, a two-mile-long fracture in a lava flow, reaches a depth of fifty feet in places and is ten to fifteen feet wide. Notice how the two opposing walls form an exact match. The crack traps cold air, and winter ice lingers in its crevices until early summer. A hiking trail explores the 1,000-year-old crack.

The byway continues south for eight miles, passing irrigated fields to Christmas Valley. The byway turns east here on a paved road and travels out to Fossil Lake, Lost Forest, and the Sand Dunes. The round-trip from the intersection is forty-four miles, and a high-clearance vehicle is needed for the last four miles. The byway heads east through green pastures and wide sagebrush flats.

Dried-up Fossil Lake, the next stop, is a veritable treasure trove of fossils from the Pleistocene Epoch of 10,000 years ago. Fossil Lake, once part of ancient Fort Rock Lake, has yielded the bones of sixty-eight bird species, including flamingos, eagles, and geese, and twenty-three mammal species, including mammoths, camels, beavers, giant ground sloths, and three horse species. The area is closed to vehicles, but visitors may walk around the 6,550-acre site.

Shifting sand dunes lie beyond Fossil Lake. The dunes, reaching sixty feet, are part of 16,000-acre Sand Dunes Wilderness Study Area. Although about 10,000 acres of the dune field remain open to off-road vehicle travel. Westerly winds, scouring Christmas Valley's dry floor, swept sand from ancient Fort Rock Lake against low ridges on the valley's east side forming the scenic dunes.

Lost Forest, a biological anomaly, grows on both the sand dunes' eastern edge and at the byway's eastern terminus. The Lost Forest Research Natural Area preserves a 9,000-acre stand of ponderosa pine growing in the middle of Oregon's high desert. Ponderosas normally require at least fourteen inches of precipitation annually to survive, but at the Lost Forest they receive only eight to ten inches. How and why they live here, isolated almost forty miles east of ponderosa forests in Fremont National Forest, is a mystery. They are probably a remnant of the vast Pleistocene forest that covered this area when the climate was wetter and cooler. A water-resistant layer of soil, possibly an old lakebed, also allows surface sand to trap and retain moisture. Lost Forest, with many primitive camping sites among the pines, makes a good base to explore the dune field. Vehicle use is limited to existing roadways to protect tree roots and prevent soil damage.

Byway travelers need to backtrack twenty-four miles along the byway route from Lost Forest to Christmas Valley to continue the tour. Christmas Valley, founded in 1961 as a retirement community, offers gas, food, and lodging. The byway turns south from Christmas Valley and heads toward the barren Black Hills. These rolling hills support two rare plants, Snowline cymopterus and Cusick's buckwheat. These low growing perennials are protected by the BLM.

The last eleven miles of the byway run southeast between the Black Hills and flat-topped, 5,630-foot Table Rock, a basalt volcanic neck. The byway ends on Oregon Highway 31, seven miles east of historic Silver Lake.

23 GALICE-HELLGATE
Oregon

General description: A paved, thirty-nine-mile, Type I byway that follows the Rogue National Wild and Scenic River from near Merlin to Grave Creek in southeastern Oregon. Another byway spur climbs from Galice into the forested Siskiyou Mountains.

Special attractions: Rogue National Wild and Scenic River, Indian Mary Park, Almeda Park, hiking, river rafting and floating, fishing, wildlife observation, jet-boating, camping.

Location: Southwestern Oregon. The byway begins at the Merlin Exit, #61, on Interstate 25, four miles north of Grants Pass. The road goes through Merlin, then parallels the Rogue River to Grave Creek. A byway spur leaves Galice and climbs west eighteen miles to the Siskiyou National Forest boundary.

Byway route names and numbers: Merlin-Galice Highway, BLM Road 34-8-36, Forest Service Road 23.

Travel season: Year-round. Snow closes the spur road west of Galice in winter.

Camping: Josephine County Parks operates two campgrounds along the byway. Indian Mary Park has ninety-five sites, showers, boat ramp, beach, and playground. Almeda Park has twenty-five sites with boat ramp, fishing access, two group camping areas.

Services: Complete services at Merlin and Grants Pass. Limited services at Galice, including boat rentals.

Nearby attractions: Grave Creek to Marial Back Country Byway, Wild Rogue Wilderness Area, Siskiyou National Forest, Kalmiopsis Wilderness Area, Grassy Knob Wilderness Area, Gold Beach, Oregon Coast, Rogue River National Recreation Trail, Valley of the Rogue State Park, Oregon Caves National Monument.

For more information: BLM, Medford District Office, 3040 Biddle Road, Medford, OR 97504. (503) 770-2411.

The trip: Set amidst the rugged, densely forested Siskiyou Mountains, the Galice-Hellgate Back Country Byway runs through a variety of terrain that includes agricultural land, a deep river canyon, and steep mountain slopes. The paved, Type I byway is two lanes from Interstate 5 to Galice. The rest of the road is single lane with scenic turnouts and passing zones. The byway can be very busy on summer weekends, otherwise traffic is generally light. Visitor information is available at the BLM's Rand Visitor Center just north of Galice.

Weather is moderate year-round in the lower elevations along the river. Expect summer temperatures as high as 100 degrees. Daily highs along the top of the byway at 4,500 feet are much cooler. Winter snowfall also closes the byway's western spur. Spring and fall are both pleasant times to drive the byway.

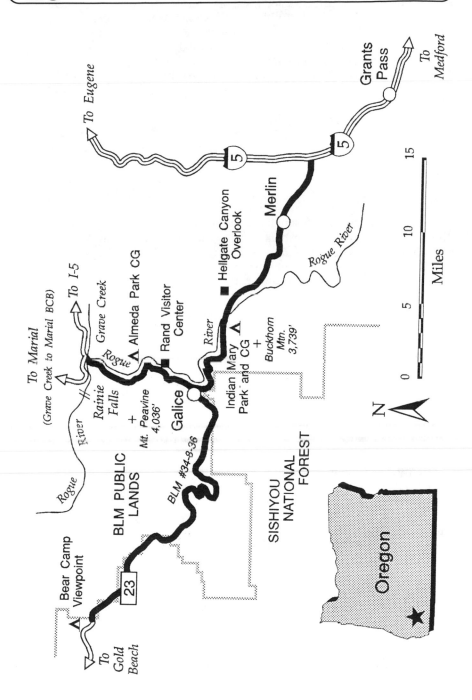

To Eugene

To Medford

Grants Pass

5

5

Merlin

Hellgate Canyon Overlook

Rogue River

Miles

To I-5

Grave Creek

Almeda Park CG

Rand Visitor Center

Rogue

River

To Marial
(Grave Creek to Marial BCB)

Rainie Falls

Mt. Peavine 4,036'

Galice

Indian Mary Park and CG

Buckhorn Mtn. 3,739'

N

BLM #34-8-36

BLM PUBLIC LANDS

Rogue River

Rogue River

SISHIYOU NATIONAL FOREST

Bear Camp Viewpoint

23

To Gold Beach

Oregon

15

10

5

0

The byway begins four miles north of Grants Pass at the Merlin Exit, #61, on Interstate 5. The road heads four miles west to Merlin. All services, including gas, groceries, and rafting outfitters, are located here. Beyond Merlin the byway passes gentle forested hills, broken by open pastures, grazing cattle and horses, and ranch homes. Four miles past Merlin the scenery changes dramatically when the byway reaches the Rogue River canyon. The next fifteen miles parallel the river as it runs through a deep rocky gorge bordered by steep, forest-clad mountains.

An eighty-four-mile segment of the Rogue River, southwestern Oregon's principal waterway, was designated one of the nation's first Wild and Scenic Rivers by Congress in 1968. The designated area, averaging one-fourth mile on each riverbank, begins at the Applegate River mouth near Grants Pass and ends near Gold Beach on the Pacific coast. The fifteen-mile-long section of the Rogue paralleling the byway is classified as a Recreational River. It is readily accessible by road, has some shoreline development, and provides a wide range of recreational opportunities. The Wild River segment runs from Grave Creek at the byway's end to Illahe. It is accessible only by boat or trail and preserves the river's primitive character.

Hog Creek Landing, a Josephine County park, is the byway's first stop along the river. This site, with a boat ramp, is the start of the most popular raft trip on the river. The fourteen-mile float from Hog Creek to Grave Creek takes six to eight hours and contains several Class I and Class II rapids. Visitors can either rent or bring their own rafts and inflatable kayaks or take guided tours down the river. Outfitters, boat rentals, and car shuttles are available in Merlin and Galice. If you float the river on your own remember to wear a life jacket, know your ability and the river, and watch for possible hazards including other boats and swimmers.

An impressive overlook lies just past Hog Creek Landing. Below the byway the Rogue River runs glassy smooth through narrow, cliff-lined Hellgate Canyon. The river has sliced down through ancient bedrock leaving this short rocky canyon. The canyon, once proposed as a dam site, was a gift of the Oregon Pacific Power and Light Company to the Wild and Scenic Rivers' system. The dramatic canyon is a favorite locale for filmmakers. Many Hollywood stuntmen have jumped or "fallen" off its cliffs into the river far below.

The byway runs west from Hellgate Canyon, past Dunn Riffle, and over a picturesque girder bridge to the river's south bank. Indian Mary Park, operated by Josephine County, sits a short distance past the bridge. The park encompasses the smallest Indian reservation ever granted by the U.S. government. Indian Mary's father, Umpqua Joe, saved white settlers from a planned massacre in the 1850s. In gratitude the reserve was given to her in 1894. Indian Mary Peters operated a ferry here for many years. It's maintained today as a recreation site with ninety-five shaded campsites, showers, a boat ramp, playground, beach, and fishing access.

Past Indian Mary Park, the byway continues west along the Rogue River. A lofty viewpoint offers a view down into rocky Taylor Creek Gorge, and several developed BLM recreation sites give river access. These sites, with picnic tables and restrooms, are good spots for fishermen to stop and cast their lines. Common fish in the Rogue include chinook salmon, coho salmon, steelhead trout, cutthroat trout, rainbow trout, shad, and sturgeon.

Hellgate Bridge spans the Wild and Scenic Rogue River on the Galice-Hellgate Byway.

Steelhead or sea-run rainbow trout are the river's best known fish. The steelhead migrate out into the ocean at two or three years of age. By their fourth year, they instinctively return to spawn in the stream where they hatched. The winter fish that return from November to March offer fishermen an almost unmatched freshwater challenge. Winter steelhead in the Rogue weigh between five and fifteen pounds, with occasional twenty pounders.

The byway turns north just before Galice and continues threading for seven miles along the Rogue River. The road, however, become narrower with blind curves. The BLM's Rand Visitor Center lies just north of Galice. Visitor information, including maps and brochures, and river permits for the Rogue's wild section are available here. The center is open daily mid-May through mid-September.

Josephine County's Almeda Bar Park has twenty-five campsites, including two group camping areas, a boat ramp, and fishing access. This is the put-in for the four-mile float trip from Almeda Park to Grave Creek. Some of the best whitewater on the Hellgate Recreation Section of the river is on this stretch. Air for rafts is available for 75 cents for five minutes.

The byway's northern terminus is where Grave Creek enters the Rogue River. The Grave Creek to Marial Back Country Byway begins at the end of the bridge over the river. A sharp left turn goes down to a boat ramp for rafters floating the Rogue's wild section and is the trailhead for the forty-mile-long Rogue River National Recreation Trail. This trail, an historic access route to mining settlements along the Rogue, is usually hiked in five days. A good day-hike travels about four miles down the trail to Whiskey Creek Cabin National Historic Site, a well-preserved 1880 miner's cabin.

Just before Galice, a left turn on Galice Road, BLM Road 34-8-36, leads travelers eighteen miles up the byway's western spur to Bear Camp Pasture on the edge of Siskiyou National Forest. The single-lane, paved road has blind corners, rock slide areas, and logging truck traffic. It is normally open from May through October. This byway branch follows the North Fork of Galice Creek. The stream twists down over rounded boulders and fallen logs, its banks thickly lined with trees and ferns.

After a few miles the road turns away from the creek and switchbacks up steep slopes. After 2,800 feet of climbing, the byway reaches 3,569-foot Soldier Camp Saddle atop the verdant Siskiyou Mountains. Great views unfold through openings in the forest canopy. To the north lies the dark cleft of the Rogue River drainage. Eastward rises the snowcapped cone of 9,495-foot Mt. McLoughlin. And to the south and west, the ridges and peaks of the Siskiyou Mountains spread like a crumpled green blanket to the horizon.

The byway edges shelf-like for three miles past the saddle on a north-facing mountainside. Impressive dropoffs fall away from the narrow road. Below stretches a patchwork of clear-cut and reforested areas managed by the BLM for wood products.

The road, traveling northwest, follows the border between BLM lands and Siskiyou National Forest. The road name becomes Forest Service Road 23. The byway winds in and out of the range crest through a dense woodland until it ends on the national forest boundary. Bear Camp Overlook lies just beyond the back country byway's end. This 4,973-foot viewpoint is a great place to stop. The vista northward into the Rogue River gorge and the Wild Rogue Wilderness Area is marvelous. A picnic table and restrooms are set among the damp forest. It's a fitting end to a spectacular drive. From here you can retrace your steps back down to Galice or continue following the scenic forest road another forty-eight miles west to Gold Coast on the Pacific shore.

General description: A Type I, thirty-three-mile road that explores the rugged mountains and canyons north of the Rogue River in southwestern Oregon.
Special attractions: Camping, hiking, backpacking, rafting, fishing, wildlife study, scenic views, Rogue River National Recreation Trail, Rogue River Wild and Scenic River, Rogue River National Historic Site, Wild Rogue Wilderness Area, Historic Kelsey Packtrail, Whiskey Creek Cabin.
Location: Southwestern Oregon. The byway begins at Grave Creek, twenty-four miles west of the Merlin exit, #61, on Interstate 5 just north of Grants Pass. Follow the Galice-Hellgate Back Country Byway (Merlin-Galice Road) along the Rogue River to its junction with Grave Creek. The byway begins across the bridge. Turn left on BLM Road 34-8-1, the Mount Reuben Road.
Byway route names and numbers: Mount Reuben Road (BLM 34-8-1), BLM 32-8-32, Kelsey Mule Road (BLM 32-8-31), Marial Road (BLM 32-9-14.2).
Travel season: Spring, summer, and fall. Snow closes the road during the winter.
Camping: Primitive camping along the byway. The BLM's Tucker Flat Campground at the byway's end on the Rogue River has primitive sites and pit toilets. Bring water or plan on purifying water.
Services: No services on byway. The nearest services are at Merlin on Interstate 5 and Grants Pass.
Nearby attractions: Galice-Hellgate Back Country Byway, Wild Rogue Wilderness Area, Siskiyou National Forest, Kalmiopsis Wilderness Area, Gold Beach, Oregon coast, Valley of the Rogue State Park, Oregon Caves National Monument.
For more information: BLM, Medford District Office, 3040 Biddle Road, Medford, OR 97504. (503) 770-2411.

The trip: The Grave Creek to Marial Back Country Byway climbs from the Rogue River's narrow gorge over the rumpled Siskiyou Mountains before dropping down to the settlement of Marial and the river again. The byway provides the only road access to the central section of the Rogue River.

The single-lane road, paved only at its beginning above the Rogue River and for a few miles on the Kelsey Mule Road, is gravel with numerous turnouts for passing and scenic views. Passenger cars can easily drive the byway. Motor homes and trailers should not attempt the route. Drivers need to take care. There are many steep hills, blind corners, and logging trucks. The road travels through remote, mountainous country. Be prepared by carrying water, food, warm clothes, and enough gas. Travelers should also stay on the byway. A network of private roads and logging roads spreads over the mountains and without an accurate map, it is easy to get lost. The round trip from Grave Creek to Marial and back is almost seventy miles. Allow four to six hours to safely drive the byway.

The best seasons to travel the byway are summer and fall. Summer visitors should expect hot days, with temperatures as high as the nineties along the river. Temperatures are cooler at 3,500 feet on the byway's upper elevations.

Autumn days are pleasantly warm with cool nights. The byway closes in winter due to heavy snowpack.

The byway begins on the north side of the bridge over the Rogue River at its junction with Grave Creek twenty-four miles west of the Merlin exit, #61, on Interstate 5 just north of Grants Pass. The byway is accessed via the Galice-Hellgate Back Country Byway paralleling the Rogue River. The 1846 grave of fourteen-year-old Martha Leland Crowley, daughter of a pioneer family, gave Grave Creek its name. The nearby community of Leland was named in her memory.

After crossing the bridge, make a left turn on the Mount Reuben Road, BLM Road 34-8-1. Below the byway here lies a boat ramp for rafters embarking on the Rogue River's wild section and the trailhead for the forty-mile-long Rogue River National Recreation Trail. The well-constructed trail borders the river between Grave Creek and Illahe. Backpackers usually take five days to walk the trail, explore side canyons, and discover the area's rich animal and plant life.

The paved byway climbs steeply out of the river canyon, winding shelf-like along the northern slopes. The first pulloff gives an impressive view of Grave Creek Falls. The ceaseless roar of the river boiling through the chute drifts up to the overlook. Rainie Falls, a twenty-foot waterfall, lies below another viewpoint just up the road. Its frothy whitewater plunges down the narrow riverbed, while ant-like rafters portage and line their boats along the river's north bank.

After six serpentine miles, the byway leaves the Rogue canyon behind and turns onto the western flank of Mount Reuben. This winding section of the byway was constructed by the Civilian Conservation Corp in the 1930s. A 1.5-mile trail leads from the byway to the abandoned fire lookout on Mount Reuben's summit.

For an interesting side-trip, turn west off the byway where the pavement ends and drop into Whiskey Creek. A one-mile trail following an old road leads to a remote miner's cabin built around 1880, the oldest known standing cabin in the lower Rogue River canyon. It was later inhabited by Lou Martin until his death at eighty-three in 1977. Today it is owned by the BLM and listed on the National Register of Historic Places.

The byway, threading along steep mountainsides, offers spectacular views of the rugged Siskiyou Mountains. Ridges and peaks, densely clad with pine and fir, tower above deep canyons. The road passes through both clear-cut and reforested sections. The byway eventually reaches Ninemile Saddle, a high divide on the paved, one-lane Kelsey Mule Road, separating the Rogue River and Umpqua River drainages. There are several primitive campsites along here. A branch road heads west via BLM and Forest Service roads to the coast.

The Marial Road, BLM Road 32-9-14.2, turns southwest from 3,284-foot Fourmile Saddle and descends 2,500 feet down to Marial on the Rogue River. The byway traverses a well-managed forest, with clear-cut areas, reforested sections, and old-growth forest. The road passes through several dark, damp forests filled with towering western redcedar and Douglas fir. Rhododendron, Oregon grape, salmonberry, and ferns line rushing streams and summer wildflowers carpet open meadows. Mammals living along the byway include black-tailed deer, Roosevelt elk, and black bear. The Rogue is also the northern-most range of the ringtailed cat, a desert animal. Hikers will see lizards, skinks,

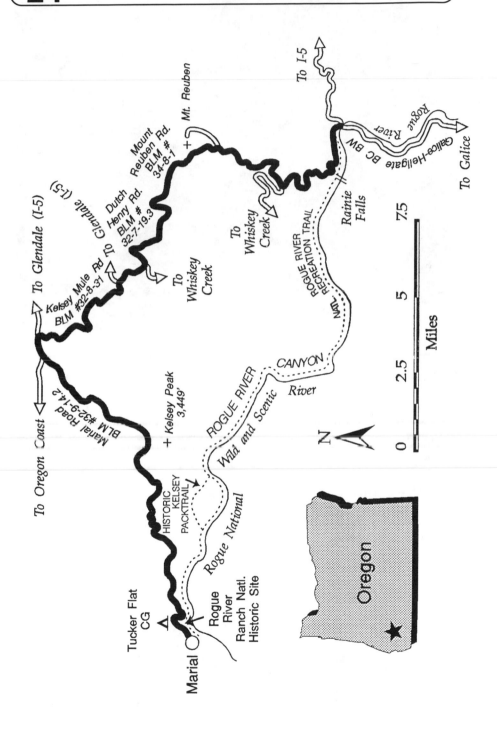

To I-5

Rogue River

Galice-Hellgate BC BW

To Galice

Mt. Reuben

Mount Reuben Rd. BLM # 34-8-1

Dutch Henry Rd. BLM # 32-7-19.3

To Glendale (I-5)

To Glendale (I-5)

Kelsey Mule Rd BLM #32-8-31

To Whiskey Creek

To Whiskey Creek

Rainie Falls

ROGUE RIVER RECREATION TRAIL

NAT'L

7.5

To Oregon Coast

Marial Road BLM #32-9-14.2

+ Kelsey Peak 3,449'

ROGUE RIVER

Wild and Scenic

CANYON

River

5

2.5

N

0

Miles

HISTORIC KELSEY PACKTRAIL

Rogue National

Tucker Flat CG

Rogue River Ranch Natl. Historic Site

Marial

Oregon

The Rogue River plunges through Grave Creek Falls below the Grave Creek to Marial Byway.

and salamanders, and less frequently, rattlesnakes, king snakes, and ring-necked snakes.

The Historic Kelsey Packtrail, the principal route through the Rogue River Canyon from the 1850s until the present Rogue River Trail was built, lies below Bald Ridge, site of a 1930s CCC camp. Sections of the old trail have been converted to roads, but the segment from Kelsey Creek to Quail Creek still exists as an historic trail. It is accessed from the main Rogue River Trail upriver from Marial.

Near the canyon bottom, the byway passes the BLM-administered Rogue River Ranch National Historic Site. The large, two-story house was built by the pioneer Billings family in 1903. Between 1903 and 1930, the Billings Trading Company at the ranch was the canyon's social center for the region's 100 or so residents. The nearby town of Marial was named for George Billings' daughter Marial, born here in 1898. The ranch was sold in 1931 and used as a vacation retreat until the federal government acquired it in 1970.

Tucker Flat Campground, with campsites and pit toilets, lies just beyond the ranch along Mule Creek. The creek was named in 1852 when a detachment of soldiers lost a mule named John along the stream. It was first called John Mule Creek, but later shortened to Mule Creek. The wayward mule was found several years later. Mule Creek forms the northeastern border of the Wild Rogue Wilderness Area. A trail climbs up the West Fork of scenic Mule Creek from the campground. The historic Mule Creek Mining District was centered in the canyon, and evidence of the search for gold abounds.

Tucker Flat also makes a great basecamp for day-hiking the Rogue River Canyon. Just downstream lies the torrent of Mule Creek Canyon. The Rogue, trapped in the narrow, rock-walled canyon, dives through a series of tricky rapids called White Snake, Narrows, and Coffee Pot. It's a good place to sit and watch rafts careen through the heavy whitewater.

About six miles upstream from Tucker Flat on the Rogue River Trail is Wrinkle Bar, one of western novelist Zane Grey's favorite places. He based a novel, *Rogue River Feud*, here, and bought a small log cabin. He once wrote of Wrinkle Bar, "I was content to walk around under the oaks and pines, to breathe the fragrance of the forest once more, to listen to the singing river, to watch the flight of wild fowl and hawks, and to gaze long at the sunset-flushed clouds above the lofty peaks in the west."

The byway ends just past Tucker Flat at Marial alongside the river. Overnight lodging is available at Marial Lodge. The town sent and received its mail as late as 1963 by mule and horse to and from Agness downstream and then by boat to Gold Beach on the coast. A pioneer cemetery sits near the end of the road. The Marial Archaeological Site, one of western Oregon's oldest human habitation sites, is nearby. From Marial, the traveler must climb back up the steep Marial Road and follow the byway's winding thread back to Grave Creek.

25 LESLIE GULCH-SUCCOR CREEK
Oregon

Description: A fifty-two-mile drive through barren desert canyons and over sagebrush-covered plateaus. The byway offers spectacular views and unique geologic formations.

Special Attractions: Succor Creek State Recreation Area, Lake Owyhee, Leslie Gulch, hiking, fishing, rockhounding, backpacking, outstanding views, wildlife study, camping.

Location: Southeastern Oregon near the Idaho border. The byway begins about forty miles south of the Vale, Ontario, and Interstate 84 area, or eighteen miles north of Jordan Valley on U.S. 95.

Byway route names: Succor Creek Road, Leslie Gulch Road.

Travel season: Mid-April through October. The byway is not maintained during the winter when snow and mud close the roads. Heavy summer thunderstorms and flashflooding can make the roads temporarily impassable.

Camping: Succor Creek State Recreation Area has nineteen primitive sites. A fee is charged. The BLM has a twelve-site primitive campground at the bottom of Leslie Gulch by Lake Owyhee.

Services: All services are available at Jordan Valley, Vale, Nyssa, and Ontario. Fill your gas tank and carry sufficient supplies and water when driving the byway.

Nearby attractions: Lake Owyhee State Park, Owyhee Wild and Scenic River, Owyhee Uplands Back Country Byway, Oregon Trail ruts, Jordan Craters.

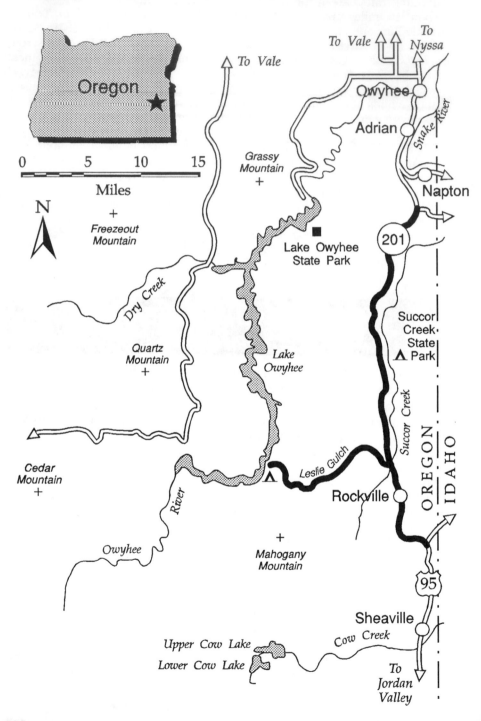

Oregon

To Vale

To Vale

To Nyssa

Owyhee

Adrian

Snake River

Napton

201

0   5   10   15

Miles

N

Grassy Mountain
+

Freezeout Mountain
+

Lake Owyhee State Park

Succor Creek State Park

Dry Creek

Quartz Mountain
+

Lake Owyhee

Succor Creek

Cedar Mountain
+

River

Leslie Gulch

Rockville

OREGON | IDAHO

Owyhee

Mahogany Mountain
+

95

Sheaville

Upper Cow Lake

Lower Cow Lake

Cow Creek

To Jordan Valley

For more information: BLM, Vale District Office, 100 Oregon Street, Vale, OR 97918. (503) 473-3144.

The trip: The Leslie Gulch-Succor Creek Back Country Byway travels through some of Oregon's wildest landscapes. It wends through deep, scenic canyons, past strangely carved rock formations, and over high, rolling plateaus that offer wide vistas.

The road is mostly one-and-a-half lanes, gravel, and regularly maintained in summer. Passenger cars, under normal conditions, can drive the entire byway with care. A high-clearance vehicle is recommended when the road is rough or temporarily washed out. Larger recreational vehicles or trailers should not drive the winding Leslie Gulch Road with its sustained 10% road grade. The total byway length, including the round trip through Leslie Gulch, is sixty-eight miles. Allow three to four hours to drive the entire route.

The byway is generally open from mid-April through October. Snow and mud close the route during the winter months. April and May are pleasant times to drive the road, but be cautious of wet, muddy road conditions. Temperatures are moderate, usually between sixty and eighty degrees, and wildflowers spread a colorful carpet across the barren desert in May and early June. Summers are hot. Expect daily highs in the nineties or low 100s.

The byway begins about eight miles south of Adrian on Oregon Highway 201 or seven miles east of Homedale, Idaho. Here the Snake River makes a slight bend into Oregon before becoming the border of Oregon and Idaho. Farms and ranches fill the river's floodplain with a patchwork of fields, while stately cottonwoods line the wide river. Crops grown here include corn, sugar beets, wheat, alfalfa, onions, potatoes, and fruits. The byway's first mile passes farmland, before traversing low, swelling hills covered with scattered sagebrush, saltbush, shadscale, and clumps of bunch grasses.

After eleven miles, the road reaches a divide. Owyhee Ridge, studded with sharp volcanic crags, rims the western skyline. Succor Creek slices through an abrupt canyon to the south, and the byway's dusty thread drops steeply down to its mouth and enters Succor Creek State Recreation Area. No one is sure how the creek got its unusual name, but locals tell two versions. One says that early pioneers found succor or aid there from thirst. The other says early miners in this gold-barren region were suckers. An 1895 stage stop in the canyon spelled the name "Sucker."

The byway wends along Succor Creek as it gurgles over rounded boulders and glides through deep pools. Its banks are lined with alders, willows, and occasional cottonwoods. Ragged cliffs, carved by erosion into buttresses, aretes, and spires, tower overhead. The cliffs are volcanic tuff deposited from explosive eruptions about fifteen million years ago. Other rocks found here include obsidian, calcite crystals, petrified wood, and the thunderegg, Oregon's state rock. The thunderegg, usually about the size and shape of a tennis ball, is filled with sparkling crystals of agate and quartz. After five miles the byway passes the nineteen-site state park campground. Sites are primitive, although water is available.

South of the campground, the byway begins climbing out of the canyon. There are spectacular views into a steep 200-foot-deep, cliff-lined gorge below and north into the narrow aperture of Succor Creek Canyon. The byway continues traversing upward and reaches a high divide surrounded by gentle mountains capped by dark basalt rimrock. Ten miles from the campground

Rugged cliffs tower over Succor Creek along the Leslie Gulch-Succor Creek Byway in Oregon.

the byway reaches the turnoff to Leslie Gulch.

The sixteen-mile Leslie Gulch Road is not recommended for travel by larger motorhomes or trailers. Steep, winding, and continuous grades of 10% are encountered in the upper canyon. The gravel road is in excellent condition. The Leslie Gulch byway section begins by passing through tawny brown hills with sweeping vistas over the wild Owyhee uplands of southeastern Oregon.

After reaching the byway's high point at about 4,800 feet, the road plunges eight miles down Leslie Gulch to Lake Owyhee. The gulch is named for pioneer rancher Hiram E. Leslie, who was killed by lightning here in 1882. Leslie Gulch is a narrow canyon filled with weirdly eroded cliffs, flying buttresses, minarets, gargoyles, arches, and pinnacles that soar over the byway. The rock, called Leslie Gulch Tuff, is a 1,000-foot-thick rhyolite ash-flow tuff deposited when Mahogany Mountain to the southwest erupted and spilled a molten froth over the surrounding countryside.

Many animal species live in the scenic canyon. Mule deer and a growing population of California bighorn sheep roam the rocky hillsides. Raptors, including eagles, hawks, owls, and vultures, ride the spacious sky overhead. Other birds seen include Chukar partridge and dove. Hikers should be wary of rattlesnakes among fallen rocks and boulders. Leslie Gulch also supports two rare plant species that are endemic to the canyon, Packard's blazing star and Etter's grounsel. A stand of ponderosa pine grows in a side-canyon, a possible remnant of forests that covered the region over 10,000 years ago.

Numerous pullouts along the canyon byway allow stops for photography and sightseeing. Rough, boulder-choked canyons branching off from Leslie Gulch invite hikers to find secret places full of wind, birdsong, and silence. The road ends on the east shore of placid Lake Owyhee, a fifty-three-mile-long reservoir that backs up the Owyhee River. There is a boat ramp and twelve-site primitive campground with vault toilets at road's end. The lake offers excellent fishing for bass and crappie.

The byway climbs back up Leslie Gulch, with its sustained grades, to the turnoff on the Succor Creek road. The route turns south and after two miles reaches a ranch and the abandoned site of Rockville. The historic Rockville School, all that's left of the community, operated from 1877 to 1969. It is now privately owned. The last eight miles of the byway goes south over rounded hills covered with sagebrush and grass, before ending in a fertile, green pasture alongside U.S. 95 a few miles west of the Idaho border. Jordan Valley lies eighteen miles south on U.S. 95.

26 LOWER CROOKED RIVER
Oregon

General description: A forty-three-mile, Type I byway through the scenic Lower Crooked River canyon and across a high desert in central Oregon.
Special attractions: Wild and Scenic Crooked River, trout fishing, hiking, camping, scenic views, wildlife.
Location: South of Prineville in central Oregon. The byway begins on Main Street in downtown Prineville and heads south on Oregon State Highway 27. The southern access is thirty miles east of Bend on U.S. 20. Turn north on Oregon 27.
Byway route number: Oregon State Highway 27.
Travel season: Year-round, although the gravel portion may be muddy after snow.
Camping: A BLM campground is at Chimney Rock Recreation Site seventeen miles south of Prineville. Nine primitive campgrounds with thirty sites are on BLM land along the byway in the canyon. Other camping is at Ochoco State Park (twenty-two sites) seven miles east of Prineville on U.S. 26 and at Prineville Reservoir State Park seventeen miles southeast of Prineville (seventy sites including full hook-ups).

Services: Complete services are in Prineville.

Nearby attractions: Ochoco State Park, Ochoco State Wayside Park, Prineville Reservoir State Park, Mill Creek Wilderness Area, Ochoco National Forest, Smith Rock State Park, John Day Fossil Beds National Monument, South Fork John Day River Back Country Byway, Christmas Valley Back Country Byway.

For more information: BLM, Prineville District, 185 E. Fourth Street, Prineville, OR 97754. (503) 447-4115.

The trip: The Lower Crooked River Back Country Byway follows a spectacular river canyon alongside the Crooked Wild and Scenic River and crosses hilly sections of Oregon's high sagebrush desert. The Type I byway offers excellent fishing, magnificent views, quiet camping, and a chance to explore some of Oregon's best BLM lands.

The byway's first twenty-one miles from Prineville to near Prineville Reservoir is a paved, two-lane road with numerous scenic pullouts. The remaining section is an all-weather gravel road that often becomes washboarded during the summer. Use caution on the road's many sharp curves, particularly during busy summer weekends. Livestock may also be on the gravel segment. The byway is suitable for passenger cars. Allow two to three hours to drive the byway one-way.

Central Oregon's weather is generally moderate. Summer visitors can expect a temperature range from fifty to ninety degrees. Both spring and fall are mild with temperatures falling between thirty and seventy degrees. Long periods of rain are infrequent. Winters are cold, with occasional sub-zero temperatures.

The byway begins on Main Street in downtown Prineville, an old ranching community that prides itself as being the "West's last frontier." Prineville, central Oregon's first real town, was founded in 1877 on Barney Prine's ranch along an early stage route. In the 1880s the town was well-known for its quick, vigilante-style justice. The town nestles in the wide valley of the Crooked River, surrounded by rimrock-capped mesas and green paddocks and hay fields watered by irrigation. In summer, it hosts the Crooked River Roundup Rodeo and the Central Oregon Timber Festival.

Ochoco State Wayside Park, a day-use area one mile west of Prineville on U.S. 126, offers scenic views of the Prineville Valley. Ochoco State Park, lies seven miles east of town off U.S. 26. Prineville Reservoir State Park, sits seventeen miles southeast of Prineville.

The byway heads south on Main Street from Prineville, past the fairgrounds, and out into a wide, flat valley rimmed by basalt cliffs on the west and rolling volcanic hills on the east. Ranches and hay fields line the byway and the meandering Crooked River for the first six miles.

Past Stearns Butte, a prominent landmark east of the byway, the canyon walls begin closing in. The river flows placidly through the steep-walled gorge. Black basalt cliffs, deposited between forty-five and thirty-five million years ago as lava flows from a chain of volcanos that include today's Ochoco Mountains, line the canyon rim. Speedy swifts and swallows wing their way against the cliffs, while hawks soar silently overhead. Western junipers forest the canyon slopes below the cliffs. Willows and shrubs densely line the riverbank.

After a few miles, the canyon briefly widens before narrowing down again. The next eight-mile river section to the dam was added to the National Wild and Scenic River system in 1988. Another seven-mile segment downstream

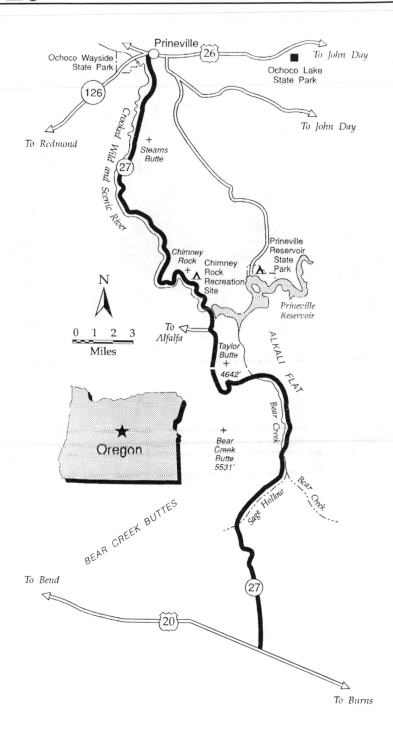

A palisade of basalt cliffs is reflected in the Lower Crooked River, a National Wild and Scenic River, alongside the Lower Crooked River Byway.

in Smith Rock State Park is also part of the system. The Wild and Scenic Crooked River is classified as a recreational river. It is managed to provide for a wide range of outdoor recreation opportunities on the free-flowing river.

The spectacular cliffs towering above the river and the byway here are called The Palisades. The road threads along cliff edges while the river spins through wide bends below. Chimney Rock Recreation Site, seventeen miles from Prineville, has primitive camping along the river. Fishing for native rainbow trout in late spring and early summer when river flows are high is excellent along the upper river. Later in the season, irrigation demands on Prineville Reservoir drop the river level to minimum flows, as low as 200 cubic feet per second.

Visitors can sight mule deer grazing along the river, coyotes, hawks, owls, eagles, and occasional black bears. Bald eagles winter in the area. Hikers should be alert for rattlesnakes among the broken boulders and scree on the canyon sides. Tall ponderosa pine lift their stately canopies over the river in the upper canyon.

A few miles past Chimney Rock the byway climbs out of the gorge and crosses 245-foot-high Arthur R. Bowman Dam, an earthen dam built in 1962 for irrigation water storage. The road, now gravel, heads south up a dry, rocky canyon to a rolling mesa above. This high, juniper-covered land offers long views. Far to the west, rimming the horizon, tower a line of snowcapped peaks in the Cascade Range, including the Three Sisters west of Bend. Taylor Butte to the east and rounded Bear Creek Butte to the south lie closeby.

The byway swings east below Bear Creek Butte and drops into a wide canyon chiseled out by Bear Creek. The byway borders trickling Bear Creek as it swings across the wide sagebrush-and-cattle-covered canyon floor. Broken basalt crags and scattered juniper are sprinkled across the hillsides. After a few miles, the dusty road bends southwest away from Bear Creek and follows a shallow, narrow canyon called Sage Hollow up to a flat sagebrush steppe that stretches south five miles to the byway's end on U.S. 20. A right turn leads thirty-four miles to Bend, central Oregon's largest town.

27 LOWER DESCHUTES RIVER
Oregon

General description: A thirty-six-mile, paved and gravel, Type I and II byway that parallels the Deschutes River in the bottom of a deep gorge in north-central Oregon.

Special attractions: Sherars Falls, Beavertail Recreation Area, Macks Canyon Recreation Area, rafting, fishing, hiking, wildlife observation, camping.

Location: North-central Oregon, about forty miles south of The Dalles. The byway runs along the east bank of the Deschutes River from seven miles south of Maupin to twenty-nine miles north. Nine miles north of Maupin, the byway is intersected by Oregon Highway 216. Maupin is on U.S. 197 between The Dalles and Madras.

Travel season: Year-round.

Camping: Developed BLM campgrounds at Macks Canyon Recreation Area and Beavertail Recreation Area. There are fourteen primitive campgrounds with about seventy-five sites along the river.

Services: All services are available in Maupin.

Nearby attractions: White River State Park, Deschutes River Recreation Area, Columbia River, The Dalles, Mt. Hood.

For more information: BLM, Prineville District Office, 185 E. Fourth Street, P.O. Box 550, Prineville, OR 97754. (503) 447-4115.

The trip: The byway follows the Deschutes River's east bank for thirty-six

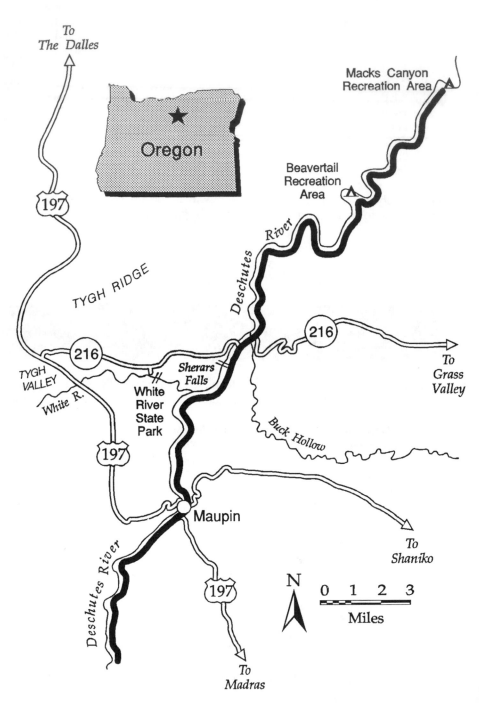

miles at the bottom of a deep, twisting canyon carved into the ancient lava flows of the immense Columbia River Plateau. Recreation for byway travelers includes rafting, fishing, hiking, and camping. The double-lane byway is paved for the nine miles between Maupin and Oregon Highway 216, with the rest of the route an all-weather gravel road. Numerous scenic pullouts allow river access. The gravel road sections become very washboarded in summer. Caution is necessary, particularly on busy summer weekends, on the road's narrow, sharp corners. Livestock is also present along the byway. Trailers are not recommended on the upriver segment from Maupin; the turn-around at road's end is tight. Visitors should allow two to three hours to drive the entire byway.

Summer visitors can expect hot, dry weather along the byway. Daily highs often climb to 100 degrees. Spring and autumn temperatures range from fifty to eighty degrees. Winters are generally cold and dry, with infrequent snowfalls. The byway is open year-round. There are often extreme fire conditions in the canyon during the summer.

There are two access points on the byway. One is from Oregon Highway 216 and the other at Maupin on U.S. Highway 197. Most visitors will embark on their byway journey at Maupin, forty-one miles south of The Dalles on the Columbia River. The pioneer Maupin family established a ferry here on the Deschutes River in 1872. All services are available in Maupin, including rafting outfitters.

The upriver section of the byway runs south from Maupin for seven and a half miles to the road's end. The canyon, capped by an erosion-resistant basalt caprock, is wide with gently contoured sides broken by sharp rock outcrops. The tawny hillsides are coated with dry grasses and a sprinkling of scrubby junipers.

The road, paralleling the river, has pullouts for fishermen and about midway up the road, a boat access point. Fishing, particularly for rainbow trout and steelhead, is very good. Other common fish species include Chinook salmon, coho salmon, mountain whitefish, and northern squawfish. This is also a popular river run, with Boxcar Rapids being the only major whitewater above Maupin. It's a good spot to sit on the cliffs jutting into the current to watch rafters bounce through the frothy waves. Campers can find some primitive sites without any amenities along the river.

The main byway section follows the east bank of the Deschutes River north from Maupin for twenty-nine miles to its terminus at Macks Canyon Recreation Area. The first nine miles to Oregon Highway 216 at Sherars Falls are paved. The remainder is gravel and is often rough and washboarded.

The byway heads north from Maupin through a wide, shallow canyon. The Deschutes River, named "Riviere Des Chutes" or River of the Falls by Hudson Bay trappers in the early 19th century, was added to the National Wild and Scenic River system in 1988. The Deschutes River Recreation Lands, managed by the BLM, borders the river. A handicapped fishing area with a wheelchair ramp lies three miles north of Maupin.

Nine miles from Maupin the byway passes spectacular Sherars Falls. Here the river funnels down a narrow chute, its boiling water dropping about fifteen feet over a bench of hard basalt. A fish ladder, carved into the rock on the west bank, allows spawning salmon an easy trail upstream. Much of the area around the falls is owned and managed by the Warm Springs Confederated Tribe. The Indians still use the ancient fishing ground to catch salmon from

A fisherman tries his luck in a raging rapid on the Lower Deschutes River Byway.

wooden platforms perched above the rushing river. The unrunnable falls are off-limits to boaters and kayakers. They must takeout before reaching the rapids.

Just downstream from the falls is Sherars Bridge, now crossed by Oregon Highway 216. An old Indian trail originally forded the narrow river here. Later pioneers floated their wagons across. In 1845 200 wagons of immigrants, led by mountain man Stephen L. Meeks, took a supposedly faster and safer route from Fort Boise to the settlements in the Willamette Valley. The party became lost in the eastern Oregon desert, and after sickness and death they finally found the Deschutes River. They crossed at Sherars Falls and headed north over the barren mesatops to The Dalles. The first bridge was built over the river in 1860 and ten years later J.H. Sherar acquired the property. He built a thirteen-room hotel and livery stable along the river, and improved the toll road through the canyon.

Oregon Highway 216 affords easy access to the Lower Deschutes River byway from U.S. Highway 197 to the west and U.S. Highway 97 to the east. A good sidetrip leaves the byway and climbs west up 216 for three miles to White River State Park. This picturesque parkland sits on the upper edge of the Deschute gorge. Westward lie rolling hills and ranches that sprawl over the wide valleys. The White River flows west along cottonwood-lined banks. At the park the river plunges seventy-five feet over a rock bench and crashes on jagged boulders. Below the river rushes through a steep canyon to the Deschutes.

The road becomes gravel where Oregon Highway 216 turns east. The canyon deepens, its rim rising over 700 feet above the byway. Here, the river follows entrenched meanders, with the long, looping bends of an old river. At one time, probably a few million years ago, the Deschutes was a placid, meandering river that weaved across soft sediments atop the Columbia Plateau. As the river began cutting into the plateau's hard, erosion-resistant basalt layers, its meanders became trapped, firmly entrenched in the volcanic bedrock. The river had nowhere to go but to follow its ancient course downward.

The walls of the lower Deschute River canyon lie open like a geology textbook. Layers of basalt, forming stairstepped cliffs, lift up from the byway to the canyon rim. Each layer records a separate massive lava flow that spread across the land. The Columbia Plateau, an area of more than 200,000 square miles in Oregon, Washington, and Idaho, was flooded by basalt lava flows that transferred over 100,000 cubic miles of volcanic material to the surface. The flows in the Deschute's canyon erupted between fifteen and twenty million years ago.

Beavertail Recreation Area, twelve miles downstream from Sherars Bridge, has twenty campsites, pit toilets, and a boat launch. The area sits on the inside edge of a great looping meander. The canyon walls rise steeply across the river, its black crags broken by bands of dry, brown grass.

Cedar Island sits in the river channel just downstream. Its name comes from the few incense cedars that grow on the island. The tree commonly occurs in the Cascade Range west of here. This is probably a relict stand left over from a wetter climate. A great blue heron rookery on the island is also of interest.

The byway continues north along the river, passing several draws, Rattle-snake and Box Elder Canyons, that offer short scenic hikes. Walkers should be wary of rattlesnakes, they are plentiful in the canyon. Other commonly seen wildlife include mule deer that browse on the short grasses, kingfishers, osprey, and chukar partridge.

Seven miles from Beavertail, the byway ends at Macks Canyon Recreation Area. A fifteen-site BLM campground and boat launching area sit along the river. The remains of an ancient Indian village lies nearby. Visitors should respect the value of the site by observing from behind the fence. Macks Canyon is a popular raft and jetboat launch site for boaters who travel the twenty-four-mile, roadless lower section of the Deschutes River to the Columbia River. There is also good hiking in Macks Canyon east of the campground area. From road's end, byway travelers must retrace the road south. The scenery looks just as good the second time.

28 NESTUCCA RIVER
Oregon

Description: An eleven-mile, Type I byway that follows the scenic Nestucca River Canyon through a lush forest in western Oregon's Coast Range.
Special attractions: Giant Douglas firs, salmon and steelhead fishing, inner-tubing, hiking, wading, photography, wildlife observation, camping, picnicking.
Location: In western Oregon's Coast Range, forty-two miles southwest of

Portland and twenty miles west of Wilsonville. The byway trip begins in Carlton, four miles north of McMinnville, off Oregon Highway 47, and ends in Beaver on U.S. Highway 101. The byway is reached from Interstate 5 by exiting at Wilsonville, Exit 283, driving west on Wilsonville Road to Newberg, then following Oregon Highway 240 for twelve miles west to Yamhill and four miles south to Carlton. The entire length of the route between Carlton and Beaver is forty-eight miles. Only eleven miles of the route, those on BLM land, have been officially designated as a Back Country Byway.

Byway route name and number: Nestucca River Access Road, BLM Road 3-6-13.

Travel season: Year-round. Snow and ice can make the road hazardous and impassable at times during the winter.

Camping: Three BLM campgrounds, Dovre, Fan Creek, and Alder Glen, are along the byway. They have tables, grates, drinking water, and comfort stations. Other campgrounds are in adjoining Siuslaw National Forest and at Cape Lookout State Park on the coast.

Services: Limited services at Carlton and Beaver. All services are available at McMinnville, Newberg, and Tillamook.

Nearby attractions: Cape Lookout State Park, Cape Meares State Park, Cape Kiwanda State Park, Staub State Park, Tillamook, Tillamook Cheese Factory, Siuslaw National Forest, Tillamook State Forest, Willamette Valley.

For more information: BLM, Salem District Office, 1717 Fabry Road, S.E., Salem, OR 97306. (503) 399-5646.

The trip: The Nestucca River Back Country Byway threads through a scenic river canyon carved by the Nestucca River in western Oregon's moist Coast Range. The byway offers an unhurried, off-the-beaten-track route between the Willamette Valley and the spectacular Oregon coast. The Type I byway is double-lane and paved, except for three miles of improved gravel road. Frequent turnouts provide river access for sightseeing and fishing.

Summer visitors can expect occasional cloudy and damp conditions in early summer, but it is usually warm and sunny. Over 120 inches of rain fall here every year, mostly between November and March. Summer daytime temperatures range from sixty to eighty degrees. Winters are cool, wet, and foggy, with snow and sleet falling on the byway's upper elevations. The road is occasionally impassable due to winter storms.

The byway's eastern access is at Carlton, an old agricultural town on the west edge of the Willamette Valley. Carlton is reached from Interstate 5 by exiting at Wilsonville, Exit 283, and driving west on twisting Wilsonville Road to Newberg, then west on Oregon Highway 240 to Yamhill. Turn south on Oregon Highway 47 in Yamhill to Carlton. Take Meadow Lake County Road west twelve miles from Carlton where it turns into the BLM's Nestucca River Access Road. This area of the Willamette Valley, a destination of the Oregon Trail immigrants 150 years ago, offers a look at well-preserved nineteenth century farms and towns. The Yamhill County Wine Tour offers travelers a chance to visit over twenty regional wineries and sample their wines.

From Carlton, the road slowly rises through oak-forested hills broken by filbert and walnut orchards, wheat fields, and grassy paddocks. Beyond the farmland, the road climbs into the lush Coast Range and crosses a 1,650-foot summit into the Nestucca River Canyon. Dropping down, the road passes dense second-generation forest and several broad clear-cut areas before

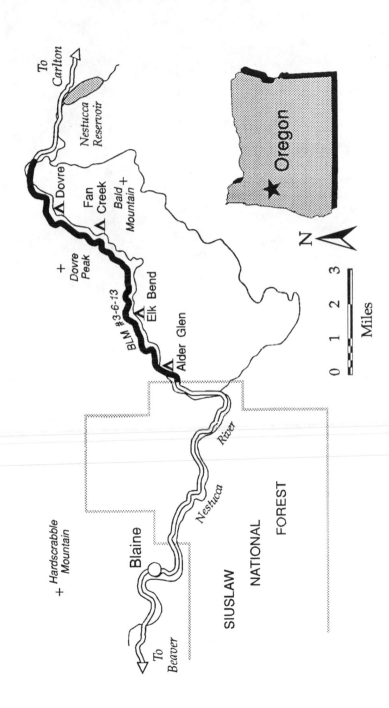

To Carlton

Nestucca Reservoir

Oregon

N

0 1 2 3
Miles

Dovre

Fan Creek

Bald Mountain

Dovre Peak

BLM #3-6-13

Elk Bend

Alder Glen

River

Nestucca

Hardscrabble Mountain

Blaine

SIUSLAW NATIONAL FOREST

To Beaver

Visitors enjoy the Nestucca River Byway in Oregon's Coast Range.

crossing onto BLM land and the byway's official start near Dovre Campground.

The eastern part of the byway wends through a narrow, meandering gorge carved by the Nestucca River in forty-million-year-old basalt, sandstone, and siltstone. The byway passes through the Nestucca Area of Critical Environmental Concern where the BLM manages the timber to protect important scenic, recreational, wildlife, botanical, and fishery values. Since 1986, the BLM has worked to improve the spawning and rearing grounds for coho salmon, chinook salmon, steelhead, and sea-run cutthroat trout in the Nestucca River and its tributaries. Informative roadside signs explain the project where byway travelers also observe the migration of the fish upstream.

A towering canopy of 200-foot-tall Douglas firs reaches high over the slender roadway on steep hillsides, interspersed with western hemlock and western redcedar. A luxuriant understory of shrubs, ferns, grasses, and wildflowers, including columbine, foxglove, and larkspur, mantle the moist soil on the slopes, while sword ferns and thick mosses crowd the road's shoulder. Red alder, black willow, and bigleaf maple thickly border the river as it tumbles over rocks and logs. The bigleaf maples are shrouded in epiphytes, such as licorice fern and club moss. Epiphytes attach themselves to the trees but are not parasitic. They take nothing from their hosts but draw sustenance from airborne moisture and nutrients.

Past Fan Creek Campground, the canyon begins to widen and gives more open views of forested and clear-cut mountainsides. Clear-cut blocks of timber, the most economical way to harvest trees, are bordered by strips of older trees. The areas, usually replanted with seedlings, help control fires and provide wildlife corridors. Over 200 animal species inhabit the Nestucca River drainage, including bald eagles, great blue herons, elk, deer, coyotes, black bears, and bobcats.

At Elk Bend Picnic Area, the river makes a lazy bend. Picnic tables and fire grates are set among the trees. This is a good place to see structures of the fisheries project, to fish, or to wade. The access road to nearby Elk Creek basin starts here.

Alder Glen Campground lies near the west end of the byway. The campground, under lofty trees, has tables, restrooms, and fire grates. A small waterfall cascades down through moss and rock into the river. At Alder Glen, the byway ends where the road crosses the river and enters Siuslaw National Forest.

Continuing west, the Nestucca River meanders across a widening valley. The road passes crumbling houses, barns, and fences of long-abandoned homesteads and modern dairy farms with gleaming equipment and green pastures. Some services, including groceries and gas, are available at Bible Creek and Blaine. Sitka spruce, a coastal tree, dominates the mountainsides above the road as it joins the Pacific Coast Highway, U.S. 101, at the logging town of Beaver.

A spectacular section of Oregon's coast lies just west of Beaver, including Cape Kiwanda State Park and Cape Lookout State Park. Cape Lookout has 250 campsites, including fifty-three with full hook-ups, picnic tables, marvelous views, a beach, and a 2.5-mile trail that winds down through a dense forest to the tip of the cape. Nearby Tillamook boasts Oregon's second most visited tourist attraction—the Tillamook Cheese Factory.

29 STEENS MOUNTAIN
Oregon

General description: A sixty-six-mile, Type II byway that climbs over 9,733-foot-high Steens Mountain, the highest peak in southeastern Oregon.
Special attractions: Camping, hiking, wildlife observation, nature study, mustang herds, backpacking, fishing, hunting, scenic views, wilderness study areas.
Location: Southeastern Oregon. The byway forms an open loop. The northern access is at Frenchglen, sixty miles south of Burns on Oregon Highway 205. The southern access begins at Frenchglen on paved Oregon Highway 205 and runs south for ten miles before turning east on the gravel Steens Loop Road.
Byway route name and number: Steens Mountain Loop Road, Oregon Highway 205.
Travel season: Summer, fall, and late spring. The road recieves minimal maintenance and may be closed in early fall due to inclement weather. Five gates along the road are used to close the road to protect it from damage in wet or snowy conditions. The upper gates are usually open by mid-July. The lower gates open by May 1.
Camping: Three BLM first-come, first-served campgrounds adjoin the byway.

Page Springs, four miles east of Frenchglen has thirty sites; Fish Lake, eighteen miles from Frenchglen, has twenty-two sites; and Jackman Park, twenty-one miles southeast of Frenchglen, has six sites and water. All three campgrounds have a $3.00 per night charge.

Services: Gas, food, and lodging are available at Frenchglen and Fields. A private campground is four miles east of Frenchglen at Steens Mountain Resort.

Nearby attractions: Malheur National Wildlife Refuge, Diamond Craters, Lakeview to Steens Back Country Byway, Hart Mountain National Antelope Refuge, Alvord Desert, Frenchglen Hotel State Wayside Park.

For more information: BLM, Burns District Office, HC 74-12533 Highway 20 West, Hines, OR 97738. (503) 573-5241.

The trip: The Steens Mountain Back Country Byway traverses over and around rugged 9,773-foot-high Steens Mountain, the highest peak in southeastern Oregon. The byway passes magical places: high tarns that reflect sky and clouds; deep gorges gouged out by glaciers; aspen-lined streams filled with solitude and birdsong; alpine meadows carpeted with summer wildflowers; bighorn sheep that cling to rocky cliffs; and scenic views that include parts of three states.

The Type II byway route includes ten miles of paved Oregon Highway 205, four miles of gravel road across Malheur National Wildlife Refuge, and fifty-two miles on the gravel Steens Loop Road. The loop road, opened in 1962, accesses over 200,000 acres of private and public land managed by the BLM as the Steens Mountain Recreation Lands. The area is managed for livestock grazing as well as recreation. The rough and rocky road is most comfortably driven in high-clearance vehicles, although passenger cars can make it with care.

The byway is open in summer and fall, although the upper elevations are generally closed until mid- to late-July due to deep snowbanks. Five gates at different elevations control access to Steens Mountain and minimize road damage. These are opened as weather and road conditions allow. If the gates are closed, travelers will have to make their byway journey one-way to the gate and back.

Summer and fall are pleasant times to travel the byway. Summer temperatures, while approaching 100 degrees in the high desert at the byway's start, are between fifty and eighty atop Steens Mountain. Like most high, isolated mountains, Steens creates its own weather. Visitors should beware of severe summer thunderstorms and lightning atop the peak. Autumn days are fair and clear, with changing aspens spreading a golden glow across the mountainsides. Heavy snowfall, beginning in October, closes the byway during the cold winter months.

The byway loop begins in Frenchglen, a old ranching community sixty miles south of Burns on Oregon Highway 205 named for local 19th century cattle baron Pete French. French's P-Ranch in Blitzen Valley became the largest single cattle ranch in the United States in the 1890s with almost 200,000 acres and 45,000 head of cattle. French was killed in 1897 by a neighbor over a land dispute. The landmark Frenchglen Hotel State Wayside Park has eight rooms and homestyle, communal meals. To make reservations call (503) 493-2825.

The road heads east at Frenchglen for four miles across 185,000-acre Malheur National Wildlife Refuge. The vast marshland of the Malheur-Harney

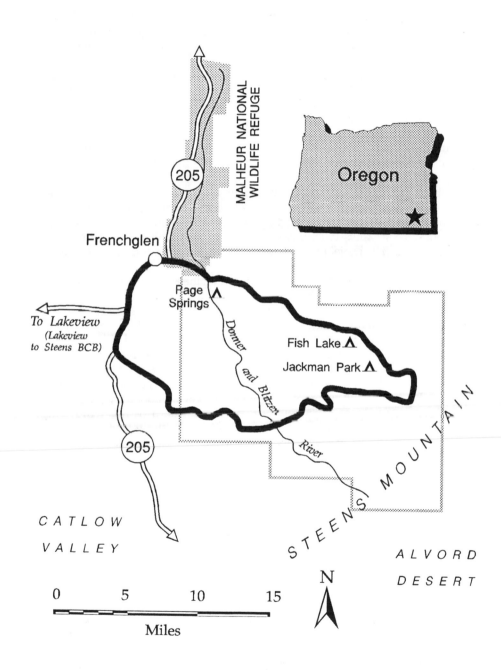

MALHEUR NATIONAL
WILDLIFE REFUGE

205

Oregon

★

Frenchglen

Page
Springs

To Lakeview
(Lakeview
to Steens BCB)

Donner

and Blitzen

Fish Lake ▲

Jackman Park ▲

River

205

S T E E N S

M O U N T A I N

CATLOW

VALLEY

ALVORD

DESERT

N

0   5   10   15

Miles

Lakes Basin, a major nesting and migration stopover for birds, was established in 1908 to stop the wholesale slaughter of birds for the millinery trade. As the byway runs past the marshes and lakes, visitors can sight over 270 bird species, including sandhill cranes, geese, ducks, trumpeter swans, ibis, egrets, and gulls.

After four miles the byway leaves the refuge and begins climbing the gradual western slope of Steens Mountain. A turn south on the Blitzen River leads to Page Springs Campground, with thirty sites, toilets, water, and firewood. Climbing eastward the roadside is coated with sagebrush and pockets of juniper, the only conifer growing on Steens Mountain other than two isolated groves of white fir.

Steens Mountain, a geological showcase of faulting and glaciation, is a thirty-mile fault-block ridge that was thrust upward some fifteen million years ago. Tilting of the block resulted in the mountain having a steep, dizzying eastern escarpment and a gentle western slope. As the precipice lifted along a north-south fault, the Alvord Basin to the east dropped over a mile below the mountain summit. Later, two glacial periods shaped the upper 2,000 feet of Steens, carving out Kiger, Wildhorse, Big Indian, and Little Blitzen gorges, and creating valleys and moraines.

Climbing higher, the sagebrush and juniper gives way to open grasslands and groves of quaking aspen. Wet meadows and lakes floor the glaciated valleys. Fish Lake Campground, surrounded by aspens, is reached after eighteen miles. The 7,300-foot area has twenty-two campsites, toilets, water, and fireplaces. Three miles further lies Jackman Park with six campsites, toilets, and drinking water.

Beyond Jackman Park lies Steens Mountain's alpine region, with deep cirques, snowfields capped by windswept cornices, and fragile alpine tundra. The plants growing in Steens different vegetational zones are unique. The mountain is a meeting place for plants from many diverse locales—the Cascade and Sierra Nevada Ranges, the Rocky Mountains, the Great Basin, and the southwest desert. Many rare and sensitive species, including Steens Mountain Paintbrush, grow on Steens' upper slopes. The BLM manages this area for its plant values.

Near the mountain top, a turnoff leads to the Kiger Gorge Viewpoint on the edge of a spectacular glacial gorge. The canyon walls, banded by cliffs, drops away from the road's end. The gorge is home to a herd of Kiger mustangs, one of the purest wild herds of Spanish mustangs in the world.

The byway continues eastward and onto the Steens crest. Grand vistas unfold from East Rim and Wildhorse Lake viewpoints of the steep, stairstepped eastern escarpment of the mountains and far below the dry alkali-lake pan of the Alvord Desert. Northward glisten Malheur and Harney lakes and beyond are forested mountains in Ochoco National Forest. To the west lie vast sagebrush-covered basins broken by sharp mesas, and on a clear day the sharp eye might see a white-capped peak in the distant Cascades.

Wildlife is plentiful on Steens Mountain. Bighorn sheep clamber over the rocky east face. Elk, mule deer, and pronghorn antelope are commonly seen grazing on the grassy western slopes. Wild mustangs range across the mountain's southern end. Beaver dam almost every stream on the west side. Many raptors live on Steens, including golden eagles, hawks, and owls. Fishermen catch rainbow and brook trout in Fish Lake, and native redband trout in the Donner and Blitzen rivers and Fish Lake. Wildhorse Lake is home to the endemic Lahontan cutthroat trout.

Turning west, the byway begins dropping down to the Blitzen River past deep

Lily Lake, a scenic subalpine tarn, lies alongside the Steens Mountain Byway.

south-facing gorges. After leaving the mountain, the road plunges into a sharp canyon lined with basalt cliffs where it crosses the Blitzen River. A few primitive campsites line the scenic river. The byway climbs steeply out of the canyon and traverses rolling volcanic hills covered with sagebrush and juniper before ending on paved Oregon Highway 205. The byway turns north here and after three miles reaches the beginning of the Lakeview to Steens Back Country Byway. The last seven miles pass cliff-lined mesas before switchbacking down to Frenchglen and the byway's end.

30 SOUTH FORK ALSEA RIVER
Oregon

Description: A Type I, eleven-mile, paved byway that follows the South Fork of the Alsea River as it drains west through Oregon's Coast Range.
Special attractions: Alsea Falls, Alsea Falls Recreation Site, Hubert McBee Memorial Park, camping, picnicking, fishing, hiking, salmon and steelhead fishing, photography, wildlife.
Location: In western Oregon's Coast Range, about thirty-five miles north-

west of Eugene between the communities of Alpine and Alsea. The eastern access is from Alpine, three miles west of Oregon Highway 99W, and via Benton County Road C-03-45120 going west from Alpine. The western access is from just south of Alsea on Oregon Highway 201 to Benton County Road C-03-48200 which joins the South Fork Alsea Access Road (BLM Road 14-6-34.1) Only eleven miles of the twenty-five-mile road, those on BLM land, are officially designated as a Back Country Byway.

Byway route name and number: South Fork Alsea Access Road, BLM Road 14-6-34.1.

Travel season: Year-round.

Camping: A fifteen-site BLM campground is adjacent to the Alsea Falls Recreation Site. There are also campsites off the byway on BLM lands.

Services: Limited services at Alsea and Alpine.

Nearby attractions: Eugene, William L. Finlay National Wildlife Refuge, Siuslaw National Forest, Oregon coastal parks and beaches, Mary's Peak Recreation Area.

For more information: BLM, Salem District Office, 1717 Fabry Road SE, Salem, OR 97302, (503) 399-5646.

The trip: The eleven-mile South Fork Alsea River Back Country Byway rises from the western edge of the Willamette Valley thirty-five miles northwest of Eugene, climbs into the Coast Range, and descends down the scenic South Fork of the Alsea River to the small town of Alsea forty miles east of U.S. 101 and the coast. The byway offers a leisurely drive, recreational opportunities in a lush river canyon, and demonstrates the BLM's multiple use management of the surrounding forest. The Type I byway is a paved, double-lane road with plenty of turnouts. The Benton County road segment west of the byway is graded gravel.

The byway, open year-round, has generally mild weather. It does, however, rain often. Annual precipitation exceeds fifty inches. Expect summer temperatures to be between sixty and eighty degrees. Winter highs fall between forty and sixty degrees, with fog and rain. Snow and sleet falls on the byway's upper elevations.

Eastern access to the byway is at Alpine, a small farming community thirty-five miles northwest of Eugene on the edge of the broad Willamette Valley. Alpine lies three miles west of Monroe on Oregon Highway 99W. From Alpine, head west of Benton County Road C-03-45120 which turns into the South Fork Alsea Access Road, BLM Road 14-6-34.1. The byway's western access is from Alsea on Oregon Highway 34. Turn south in town on Oregon Highway 201, after a mile make a left turn on Benton County Road C-03-48200, which also turns into the byway. This county road section is unpaved. Byway drivers should be alert for logging and gravel trucks along the road.

From Alpine, the road heads west past open fields and pastures bordered by clumps of trees and fences laden with salmonberry. Christmas tree farms line the roadway. About a mile past Glenbrook, the byway begins by climbing a steeply forested ridge to a high divide. There are great views west from atop the ridge across a clear-cut area into the canyon of the South Fork of the Alsea River. Rolling ridges and summits of the Coast Range, draped in emerald greenery, rise above the V-shaped canyon. The Coast Range here is composed primarily of basalt deposited fifty to sixty million years ago on

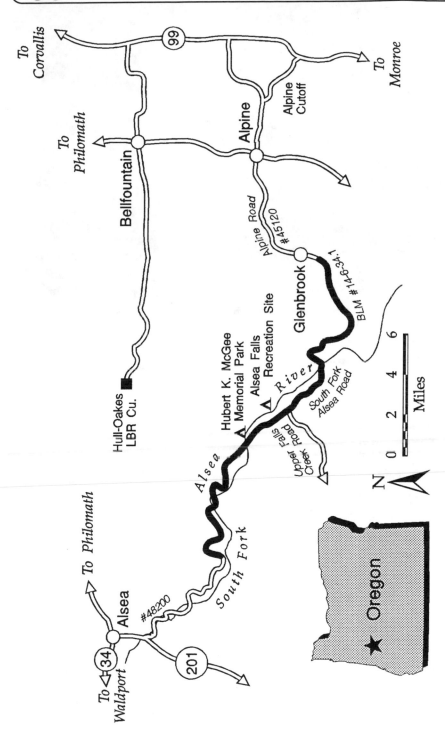

To Corvallis

To Monroe

99

Alpine

Alpine Cutoff

To Philomath

Bellfountain

Alpine Road #45120

Glenbrook

BLM #14-6-34.1

Hubert K. McGee Memorial Park

Alsea Falls Recreation Site

Hull-Oakes LBR Cu.

River

Alsea

South Fork Alsea Road

Upper Falls Creek Road

0   2   4   6

Miles

N

South Fork

To Philomath

Alsea

#48200

South Fork

34

201

To Waldport

Oregon

137

A forest canopy hems in the South Fork Alsea River Byway.

the floor of the Pacific Ocean. Layers of mudstone and sandstone, also part of the ancient seafloor, were deposited atop the basalt.

The winding byway, overhung by a dense second-growth forest, drops quickly into the canyon. After a few miles, the canyon widens and the byway reaches a sixteen-site BLM campground along the river. Just down the road is Alsea Falls Recreation Site, with a parking area, picnic tables, grills, drinking water, and vault toilets.

Alsea Falls, at the recreation site, is the byway's primary attraction. The smooth, jade-green Alsea River shatters to foam and thunder as it tumbles over a twenty-foot bench of rock and cascades down a smooth chute of water-polished basalt. Moss and ferns cling to boulders along the falls, while Douglas firs tower overhead. A trail leads through the forest to the pool at the waterfall's base.

The picnic area at Alsea Falls is a great place to explore the area's lush forest. Mild year-round temperatures, combined with generous precipitation, makes Oregon's Coast Range one of America's best environments for luxuriant plant growth. Spruce, with sharp, prickly needles, grow amidst the decaying, ancient stumps of giant Douglas firs cut long ago for lumber. Another giant tree in the forest above the Alsea River is the western redcedar. Red alder, bigleaf maple, and the brilliant colors of red vine maple line the river's course. A tangled understory of moss, sword ferns, columbines, foxglove, and larkspur carpet the forest floor.

Hubert K. McBee Memorial Park, with picnic and camping sites, lies almost

Alsea Falls lies along the South Fork Alsea River Byway.

a mile west of Alsea Falls. The park's highlight is a covered, eighty-five-foot picnic table carved from a single log.

The byway continues west following the river as it gurgles over rounded rocks and fallen logs and flows through deep, still pools. Numerous pullouts allow river access for fishermen to catch Chinook salmon, Coho salmon, and sea-run cutthroat trout. Much wildlife lives in the forest along the byway. Deer are often seen, particularly toward evening, alongside the road. Black bear, bobcats, raccoons, and skunks are more secretive. Birds seen include the raucous Steller's jay, western tanager, black-headed grosbeak, Wilson's warbler, and the chestnut-backed chickadee.

Numerous BLM side roads, including the Fall Creek Road by Alsea Falls, invite exploration. Be prepared by obtaining a detailed map of the area; it's easy to get lost in the maze of gravel logging roads.

The byway ends where the road turns to gravel. The road continues west along the widening canyon a few more miles to Oregon Highway 201 just south of Alsea. Some services, including gas and food, are available in Alsea. From Alsea, Oregon Highway 34 heads west through the scenic valley of the now wide and deep Alsea River for forty miles to Waldport on the coast. There are many state parks along the coast both north and south of Waldport.

One of the most spectacular areas is Cape Perpetua in Siuslaw National Forest about ten miles south of Waldport. Here the ocean sweeps up against a bold, ragged coastline covered by a towering spruce and fir forest. Nearby is a Forest Service visitor center with interesting displays on coastal ecology and a campground.

31 SOUTH FORK JOHN DAY RIVER
Oregon

General description: A fifty-mile, Type I and II byway that parallels the South Fork of the John Day River through a scenic canyon in central Oregon.

Special attractions: South Fork of the John Day Wild and Scenic River, camping, fishing, hiking, wildlife observation, scenic views.

Location: South of Dayville in central Oregon. The byway's northern access is Grant County 42 off U.S. Highway 26 in Dayville. The southern access is at the Malheur National Forest boundary where Grant County 68 joins Forest Road 47. This junction is accessible from Prineville via Oregon Highway 380.

Byway route numbers: Grant County 42 and 68.

Travel season: Year-round. Single-lane sections of the byway may be impassable in winter and early spring due to snow and mud.

Camping: A primitive campground is twenty-three miles south of Dayville on the byway. Tents, trailers, and motorhomes can use the site. Primitive camping is allowed along the byway on BLM land. Use existing campsites to minimize impact.

Services: Limited services are available in Dayville and Paulina, thirty-five miles west of the byway's south segment. Complete services are in John Day, thirty-eight miles east of Dayville.

Nearby attractions: Lower Crooked River Back Country Byway, Ochoco National Forest, Black Canyon Wilderness Area, Clyde Holliday State Park, John Day Fossil Beds National Monument, Picture Gorge, Malheur National Forest.

For more information: BLM, Prineville District, P.O. Box 550, Prineville, OR 97754. (503) 447-4115.

The trip: The South Fork John Day River Back Country Byway parallels the river through its scenic canyon for fifty miles from Dayville to the northern border of Malheur National Forest. The Type I and II byway offers solitude, fishing, primitive camping, hiking, and great views throughout its length.

The byway, except for a twelve-mile section near Izee on the southern

31   SOUTH FORK JOHN DAY RIVER

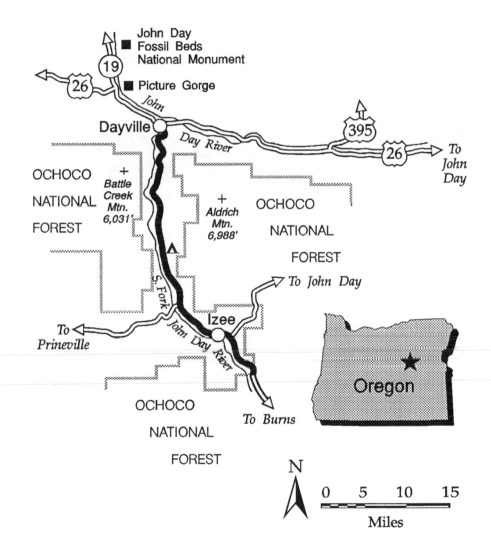

John Day
Fossil Beds
National Monument

Picture Gorge

26 **19**

John

Dayville

Day River

OCHOCO

NATIONAL

FOREST

Battle
Creek
Mtn.
6,031'

Aldrich
Mtn.
6,988'

OCHOCO

NATIONAL

FOREST

395 **26**

To John Day

To
Prineville

S. Fork John Day River

Izee

To John Day

OCHOCO

NATIONAL

FOREST

To Burns

Oregon

N

0   5   10   15

Miles

segment, is both single- and double-lane gravel road. The first ten miles south of Dayville are well-maintained by Grant County. The next twelve miles to Izee Falls is seasonally maintained by the BLM and is often impassable during the winter. Caution should be exercised on the road due to curves, washboarded sections, and livestock and wildlife on the road. The byway is easily passable in passenger cars except in winter and early spring. Byway elevations range from about 2,500 feet near Dayville to almost 4,500 feet at the byway's southern terminus. Allow three or four hours to drive the route.

Weather along the byway is moderate. Summer and early fall have pleasant daily high temperatures ranging from sixty to ninety degrees. Nights are generally cool. Expect afternoon thunderstorms, especially in July and August. Winters are cold and snowy, with temperatures often dropping below zero degrees.

The byway begins in Dayville off U.S. 26. Seven miles west of Dayville along U.S. 26 lies Picture Gorge, one of central Oregon's most unusual geologic features. Here the John Day River slices down through no fewer than seventeen distinct basalt lava flows in a deep, narrow chasm. The Sheep Rock Unit of John Day Fossil Beds National Monument lies just north of the gorge. Plants and animals, deposited in volcanic ash between thirty to forty million years ago, create one of the world's richest fossil deposits.

The byway leaves Dayville, a small ranching and logging supply center, and heads south on Grand County Road 42. The byway, bordering the small, clear river, passes several ranches spread across the canyon floor. The dry hillsides are covered with sagebrush, scruffy juniper, and scattered ponderosa pine. Thick stands of willow line the river banks.

The South Fork of the John Day River is a tributary of the 284-mile-long John Day River, one of America's longest free-flowing rivers. The river is named for John Day, a member of John Jacob Astor's party that explored the Oregon region in 1811-1812. Day and a companion, both ill, left the main party and were attacked by Indians.

A forty-seven-mile section of the South Fork of the John Day River along the byway from Malheur National Forest to just south of Dayville is part of the National Wild and Scenic River system. The segment is designated a Recreational River for its many outdoor opportunities.

After a few miles the canyon narrows. The walls on either side stairstep upwards with thick lava flows stacked on top of each other. Each layer records a violent volcanic episode in Oregon's distant geologic past. Tawny grass and sagebrush carpet the slopes between the vertical basalt cliffs. Further south the black, lichen-encrusted cliffs rise from the roadway. Ferns and moss fill lush alcoves, fed by seeping springs, in the cliff bands. Black Canyon Wilderness Area, in Ochoco National Forest, lies west of the byway up Black Canyon Creek.

Ten miles south of Dayville, the 150,000-acre Murderer's Creek Wildhorse Management Area lies east of the byway. About 100 horses roam this hilly region. Murderer's Creek Road allows access to the Aldrich Range and Ochoco National Forest east of the byway. Much wildlife lives along this remote byway, including mule deer, elk, bighorn sheep, black bear, coyotes, eagles, hawks, and chukar partridges. Rattlesnakes are common on the rocky slopes above the byway. There is excellent trout fishing in the river's clear pools.

Winding south, the byway and the river both gain elevation. The canyon becomes deeper with a high, cliffed rim. Precipitation also increases, and the juniper and sagebrush plant community is replaced by forests of tall ponderosa pines, and occasional Douglas and white firs. Grassy meadows full of wildflowers wrap the river bank with a mantle of color in summer. A primitive campground with spacious sites along the river sits twenty-three miles south from the byway's start.

Just past the Deer Creek Road, the byway steepens, narrows, and climbs the hillside above the river. The small river tumbles and cascades over smooth boulders below. Ponderosa pines tower 150-feet overhead. The canyon widens after Ellingson Mill, and the river meanders across the open valley. The byway becomes paved here as it joins Oregon Highway 380 between Prineville and John Day.

The byway follows the east bank of the South Fork as it meanders through

The South Fork John Day River Byway winds through a scenic canyon.

a wide, green valley and passes picturesque ranches. The hills along the river are no longer sharp and precipitous, but rather dry, scrubby, and covered with sagebrush.

Past the abandoned townsite of Izee, the highway bends east away from the river. The byway turns south on paved Grant County Road 68 and continues paralleling the river. A short distance below the junction the road again becomes gravel. The byway quietly ends on the Malheur National Forest boundary a few miles further south. The road, now National Forest Road 47, climbs past 6,180-foot Sugarloaf Mountain and drops down to Burns. Byway travelers can retrace the route back to Izee and follow the paved road east for forty miles to John Day.

32 FORT MEADE
South Dakota

General description: This five-mile-long, Type I byway travels through forested hills on the eastern edge of South Dakota's Black Hills near Sturgis.
Special attractions: Fort Meade, Fort Meade Cemetery, Fort Meade Museum, hiking, camping, picnicking, historic cavalry jumps, wildlife, hunting, Centennial Trail, Black Hills National Cemetery.
Location: Northwestern South Dakota. The northern access is on South Dakota State Highway 34, one-half mile east of Sturgis. The southern access is at Exit 34 on Interstate 90 just south of Sturgis.
Byway route name: Fort Meade Road.
Travel season: Year-round.
Camping: A six-unit tent campground and a six-unit horseback rider campground on the byway are open from May 15 through September 30. Other campgrounds are in nearby Sturgis and Black Hills National Forest.
Services: All services in Sturgis.
Nearby attractions: Spearfish Canyon Scenic Byway, Rapid City, Mount Rushmore National Memorial, Deadwood, Devils Tower National Monument, Black Hills National Forest, Custer State Park, Bear Butte State Park, Black Hills Passion Play, Wind Cave National Park, Jewel Cave National Monument.
For more information: BLM, South Dakota Resource Area, 310 Roundup Street, Belle Fourche, SD 57717. (605) 892-2526.

The trip: The Fort Meade Back Country Byway threads through pine-covered hills on the northeastern edge of the Black Hills, South Dakota's only mountain range, just east of Sturgis. It makes a pleasant stop for Interstate travelers, and offers hiking, picnicking, camping, and historic sites. The two-lane, gravel-surfaced, Type I byway is easily driven in a passenger car. Pullouts allow visitors to admire the scenery, go hiking, or inspect historic places. Allow thirty minutes to drive the road.

The climate on the eastern flank of the Black Hills is generally mild. Summer temperatures range from sixty to ninety degrees, with cool nights. Mornings are clear, with afternoon thunderstorms common in July and August. Autumn

Bear Butte, a sacred mountain to the Sioux Indians, looms beyond the Fort Meade Byway.

daily temperatures are between fifty and seventy. Winters are cold, with snow possible from November through April.

The byway begins on South Dakota Highway 34, about one-half mile east of Sturgis. Turn south on Fort Meade Road. Just east of the byway start lies old Fort Meade, the home of almost every U.S. Army cavalry regiment at one time or another. Civil War hero, General Philip Sheridan, selected the fort's site in 1878. The fort was named for Major General George C. Meade, the commander of the Army of the Potomac in the Battle of Gettysburg.

Fort Meade was established to quell Indian uprisings and provide protection for settlers and miners in the Black Hills. The Sioux Indians, angered by white incursions into the mountains, regarded the Black Hills as sacred. They called them the *Paha Sapa*, or "Land of Shadows." After the Indian Wars abated, the post prevented range wars and served as a training ground for the increasingly mechanized cavalry units. At its height, the fort buildings included officer's quarters, barracks, guardhouse, commissary, post office, hospital, chapel, library, bakery, ice houses, and sawmill.

During World War II the fort housed German war prisoners and was converted to a VA hospital. The VA proposed demolishing twenty-nine historic buildings at Fort Meade in 1965, but local outcry preserved the fort by placing it on the National Register of Historic Places in 1973. Today, visitors can explore the old fort and tour the Fort Meade Cavalry Museum.

Indians used the wide valley of Bear Butte Creek, where the byway begins, for centuries. Here was protection from bitter north winds, and plentiful wood, game, and water. Holes used for sharpening tools are found in boulders along

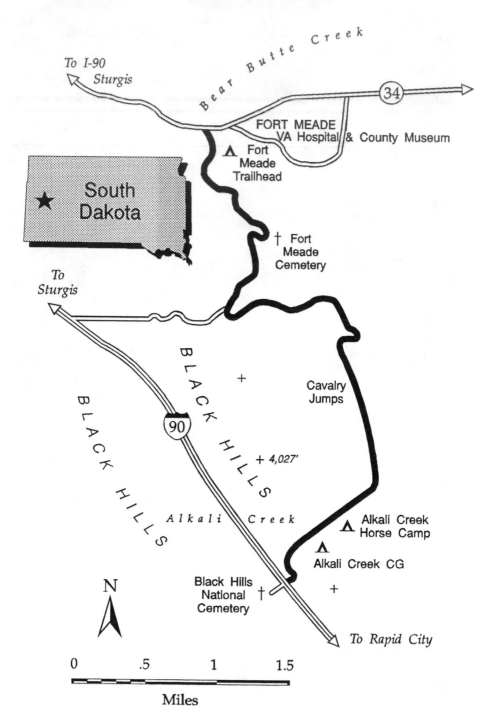

Bear Butte Creek

To I-90
Sturgis

34

FORT MEADE
VA Hospital & County Museum

Fort
Meade
Trailhead

South
Dakota

† Fort
Meade
Cemetery

To
Sturgis

BLACK HILLS

BLACK HILLS

+

I-90

+ 4,027'

Cavalry
Jumps

Alkali Creek

Alkali Creek
Horse Camp

Alkali Creek CG

Black Hills
National †
Cemetery

+

N

To Rapid City

0   .5   1   1.5

Miles

the creek. Bear Butte, a sacred Indian site just to the north, is a state park.

The byway leaves the highway and climbs south up the edge of a grassy valley. The Fort Meade Trailhead is on the east side of the road. This provides access to the 111-mile Centennial Trail that wanders the length of the Black Hills. A twelve-mile trail segment borders the byway.

Tall ponderosa pine and scrub oak line the road as it winds south. After one mile, the byway passes the old Fort Meade Cemetery perched atop an open hill. The road traverses into a lush canyon, its trickling creek densely bordered by elm, ash, and cottonwood. The byway follows the transition zone between the Great Plains that stretch eastward and the Rocky Mountains, of which the Black Hills are the easternmost extension.

After another mile the byway leaves the forest behind and enters open grasslands in a wide valley. Bear Butte pokes above the rolling prairie to the north. Historic cavalry jumps, piles of stacked stones for horses to leap, are spread across the valley floor. The valley is a good place to spot grazing mule and white-tailed deer along the forest edge on summer evenings. Other animals living here include pronghorn antelope, bobcats, coyote, porcupine, raccoons, and skunks.

At Alkali Creek, the byway swings west and heads along the forested creek. Sandstone cliff bands line the hillside north of the road. Alkali Horse Camp and Alkali Creek Recreation Site offer camping and picnic sites and a trailhead for hikers. The byway continues on another half-mile and ends at Exit 34 on Interstate 90. Black Hills National Cemetery is across the highway.

33 BULL CREEK PASS
Utah

General description: A Type III, sixty-eight-mile road that loops through the Henry Mountains in central Utah, providing scenic views of the nearby canyon country.

Special attractions: Little Egypt Geologic Site, 10,485-foot Bull Creek Pass, Mt. Ellen, Stevens Narrows, The Horn, buffalo herd, hiking, rock climbing, hunting, wildlife observation, camping, spectacular views.

Location: Central Utah, sixty-five miles south of Interstate 70. The byway's northern access is from Utah Highway 95, twenty-one miles south of Hanksville. The byway's south entrance is on Utah State Highway 276, five miles south of its junction with Utah Highway 95.

Travel season: The complete byway is open from July through October. Snow usually doesn't completely melt off Bull Creek Pass until sometime in July. Check with the BLM office in Hanksville for an up-to-date report on the road condition. The byway's lower portions near Little Egypt, Steele Bench, and Sweetwater Creek, are generally open year-round.

Camping: Developed campgrounds with sites, tables, water, and pit toilets are on the byway at McMillan Springs and just north of it at Lonesome Beaver. Two primitive areas, used by hunters, are on the Mount Pennell byway section. Primitive camping is allowed along the byway. Capitol Reef National

Park to the west has one developed campground and two primitive campgrounds.

Services: Limited services are available at Hanksville. Complete services are in Green River.

Nearby attractions: Capitol Reef National Park, Goblin Valley State Park, Canyonlands National Park, Glen Canyon National Recreation Area, Lake Powell, Burr Trail, Boulder Mountain Highway Scenic Byway, Escalante River, San Rafael Swell, slickrock and canyon hiking.

For more information: BLM, Henry Mountains Resource Area, P.O. Box 99, Hanksville, UT 84734. (801) 542-3461.

The trip: The Bull Creek Pass Back Country Byway makes an open loop that traverses the rugged and remote Henry Mountains. Spectacular views of canyons, cliffs, buttes, badlands, alpine peaks, and the surrounding canyonlands unfold from the byway as it climbs 5,000 feet over the mountains. The road is single-lane with a dirt surface. It has many steep grades and rough sections. A four-wheel drive vehicle is strongly advised for traveling the entire byway. A high-clearance truck can make the route, but it will be abused. The road is impassable during the winter and after heavy rain.

The byway and the Henry Mountains are very remote, rugged, and dry. There are no regular patrols by the BLM, and you may not meet anyone else on the road. Be prepared for every contingency when traveling the byway. Carry plenty of extra water and make sure your vehicle is in proper working condition with a full tank of gas. The road is generally unmaintained. Heavy thunderstorms in July and August can wash out road sections. Keep an eye on the weather for possible flash floods and avoid the Sweetwater drainage and Steven's Narrows in threatening weather. Use caution on the byway's many blind curves, there may be other vehicles or large rocks in the road ahead. Allow seven to nine hours to drive the route.

Due to the dramatic elevation gain from about 5,000 feet to over 10,000 feet, the byway's climate varies considerably. Summers are hot in the lower elevations, expect highs in the nineties or low 100s. It is cooler in the mountains. Thunderstorms usually occur in July and August. Autumn temperatures are more moderate and dry, with nighttime temperatures dipping to freezing in the mountains. Light snow is common from November through April in the lower elevations, with heavy snow atop the peaks closing the byway through winter.

The byway begins by turning west twenty-one miles south of Hanksville from Utah Highway 95. The dirt road bends south and skirts the edge of a high, flat-topped mesa. After two miles it passes Little Egypt Geologic Site, a fanciful assortment of eroded Entrada sandstone pillars, gargoyles, and hoodoos that reminded early cowboys of Egyptian monuments. It's a good place to stop and hike around the red rocks.

Continuing south across a sere, scrubby benchland, the byway turns west after another two miles up wide North Wash. A few cottonwoods shade the sandy arroyo. After another half-mile the byway heads north up the dry bottom of Crescent Creek. The road dips in and out of the rocky creekbed for several miles, until climbing up a steep, four-wheel drive section onto the broad outwash plain that slopes east from the Henry Mountains. The byway labors up the sloping plain, through a thick pinyon pine and juniper forest.

Partway up, the road passes the abandoned townsite of Eagle City, built

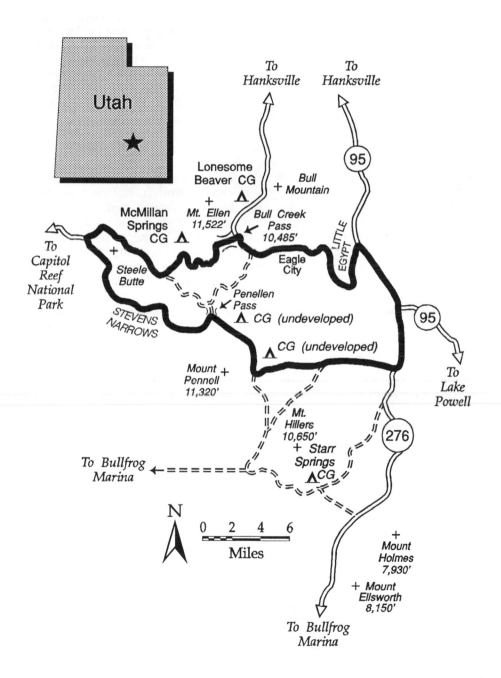

Utah

To Hanksville

To Hanksville

95

Lonesome Beaver CG

Bull Mountain

McMillan Springs CG

Mt. Ellen 11,522'

Bull Creek Pass 10,485'

To Capitol Reef National Park

Steele Butte

Eagle City

LITTLE EGYPT

STEVENS NARROWS

Penellen Pass

CG (undeveloped)

95

CG (undeveloped)

Mount Ponnell 11,320'

To Lake Powell

Mt. Hillers 10,650'

Starr Springs CG

276

To Bullfrog Marina

N

0   2   4   6
Miles

Mount Holmes 7,930'

Mount Ellsworth 8,150'

To Bullfrog Marina

in the 1890s during a minor goldrush in the Henry Mountains. Two prospectors found gold in a fissure at the head of Crescent Creek in Bromide Basin. By 1893 a small mill had been erected and over 100 men were working at a half a dozen prospects. Eagle City had several homes, a hotel, two saloons, a dance hall, three stores, and a post office. But it was not to be. The gold played out and the town was abandoned by 1900. Nothing remains today to mark the town's passing.

The byway reaches Crescent Creek's trickle after climbing almost eight miles up the slope. A thick grove of quaking aspen lines the creek and the byway, while scrub oak and ponderosa pine grow on drier hillsides above. A half-mile later the byway makes a sharp right turn toward Wickiup Pass.

The next two miles are simply awesome. The narrow byway is a spectacular shelf road that edges above a precipitous dropoff. A grassy viewpoint after the shelf road lends lofty views of Canyonlands National Park and the gorge of the Dirty Devil River to the east.

The byway continues west, dipping in and out of the Granite Ridges through spruce and fir forests that spill down steep drainages to 9,240-foot Wickiup Pass. A right turn here leads down Bull Creek to Lonesome Beaver Campground and across the desert to Hanksville. The byway turns left and switchbacks two and a half miles up to 10,485-foot Bull Creek Pass, a saddle on Mt. Ellen. The pass lies twenty miles from the byway start.

The 360-degree view from atop the pass is marvelous. Eastward lies the distant La Sal Mountains and the cliffs and buttes of the canyonlands baking under the desert sun. To the west stretches the long, shimmering Waterpocket Fold, Capitol Reef, and Boulder Mountain. A four-mile hike north along the narrow ridge from the pass leads to Mt. Ellen's 11,522-foot high point.

The Henry Mountains, named for Joseph Henry of the Smithsonian Institution by the 1869 Powell Survey, was the last named and explored range in the lower forty-eight states. The Henrys are a textbook example of what geologists call laccoliths—mountains that are formed by underground molten magma pushing up against a blanket of sandstone layers above, causing a dome-like structure in the once horizontal layers. These domes, now sharply eroded, form the five major peaks of the Henry Mountains. The upturned sandstone layers form a rim around the range's perimeter.

The byway drops steeply down the west flank of Mt. Ellen, losing 1,000 feet in about three miles. The grassy slopes of Mt. Ellen's south summit ridge tower over the road. Heading west, the byway continues losing elevation over a broad outwash plain broken by small creeks and meadows. Beyond Dry Lake Flat the road switchbacks down to Willow Spring, a small oasis surrounded by willow thickets.

McMillan Springs, the next oasis, has a BLM campground with tables, pit toilets, and running water from the spring. Tall ponderosa pines scatter across the area. There are great views west across low mesa tops to the upheaved ridge of the Waterpocket Fold.

The usually deserted campground is a good place to observe birds and other wildlife. Ravens, Clark's nutcrackers, pinyon jays, Steller's jays, nuthatches, chickadees, and towhees frequent the pine forest. Turkey vultures, kestrels, and hawks soar overhead. Mule deer are seen in the early morning and evening hours. Elk, bighorn sheep, pronghorn antelope, and mountain lion also inhabit the area, but are rarely seen.

The benches and mesa tops along the western slope of the Henry Mountains are also home to a herd of free-roaming American bison. The eighteen head transplanted from Yellowstone National Park in 1941 have flourished to a herd of over 200 animals. The Utah Division of Wildlife Resources issues a limited number of permits annually to hunt the bison. To see the bison, it's best to inquire at the BLM's Hanksville office to find out where they were last seen. If you do find the bison, remember they are dangerous wild animals.

The byway continues west down a steep, boulder-strewn road to the dry bed of South Creek. Cattle graze along the road. Grazing, part of the BLM's multiple-use policy, started in the 1870s in the Henrys, with large herds roaming the area by the 1890s. Quarrels over range rights between cattlemen and sheep owners were commonplace. Rustlers also roamed over the unpopulated area, stealing cattle and driving them into the canyons of the Dirty Devil River. Robber's Roost, one of the most famous, was an important stop on the Outlaw Trail. Fugitives included Butch Cassidy and his sidekick, Harry Longbaugh, the Sundance Kid.

The byway leaves South Creek at Steele Butte, a cliffed fortress named for early settler Pete Steele, and crosses wide Steele Bench for four miles to Sweetwater Creek. Capitol Reef National Park's Notom Road can be reached by driving across the creek and heading west. The byway turns left here and follows the broad creekbed southeast. The road, flanked by high buttes and eroded badlands, crosses the dry creek often. Scattered pinyon pine, juniper, sagebrush, and desert shrubs grow alongside the road.

Bull Creek Pass Byway follows Sweetwater Creek Valley beneath a rim of sandstone cliffs and buttes.

Slowly canyon walls begin to close in on the byway and after eight miles it enters Steven's Narrows. The non-existent road follows the fifty-foot-wide wash for a third of a mile through upturned Mesa Verde sandstone layers. The byway is extremely rough and rocky through this section. Its complexion changes with every flash flood that roars through the narrows.

Past the narrows the byway enters a valley bordered on the west by dissected walls of grey Mancos shale. Swinging south and then east, the road begins ascending a long steep section to Penellen Pass, the low saddle between Mt. Ellen and Mt. Pennell. The Horn, a towering granite buttress seamed with vertical cracks, rises south of the byway. A primitive campsite sits in a pine forest beside the byway below The Horn.

The road, now on the east side of the Henry Mountains, contours south along the forested flank of Mt. Pennell. Turkey Haven, another primitive campsite, is reached five miles from Penellen Pass. Past here the byway rapidly loses elevation and turns east down a rocky road. The vegetation changes from scrub oak, mountain mahogany, and ponderosa pine to pinyon pine, juniper, and sagebrush. Mt. Hillers rises south of the road.

Eventually the byway leaves the forest entirely, and descends into a cliff-terraced canyon carved by Straight Creek. Numerous adits or mine shafts dot the canyon walls. After crossing the creek one last time, the road climbs onto a wide bench and passes Trachyte Ranch. Just past the ranch are some eroded red sandstone domes and the byway's end on paved Utah Highway 276. A left turn leads five miles to Utah Highway 95 and Hanksville. A right turn goes to Bullfrog Marina on Lake Powell.

34 SMITHSONIAN BUTTE
Utah

General Description: A nine-mile, Type I byway that climbs above the spectacular Valley of the Virgin River in southwestern Utah. The byway offers fabulous views of Zion National Park.

Special attractions: Scenic views, picnicking, ghost town/movie set of Grafton, hiking.

Location: Southwestern Utah. The byway, twenty-six miles east of St. George and twenty-eight miles east of Interstate 15, begins in Rockville on Utah Highway 9, three miles west of Zion National Park. Its southern access is at Big Plain Junction on Utah Highway 59, sixteen miles southeast of Hurricane.

Byway route name: Smithsonian Butte Road.

Travel season: Year-round. The byway is passable to two-wheel drive vehicles in good weather. Mud from snow in winter or heavy summer thunderstorms can make travel hazardous, particularly on the steep section below Wire Mesa.

Camping: Primitive camping is allowed along the byway on BLM land; there are a few spots on both Wire Mesa and Grafton Mesa. Zion National Park has two large, shady campgrounds along the Virgin River four miles east of the byway's northern access. Springdale, on the park boundary, has full-

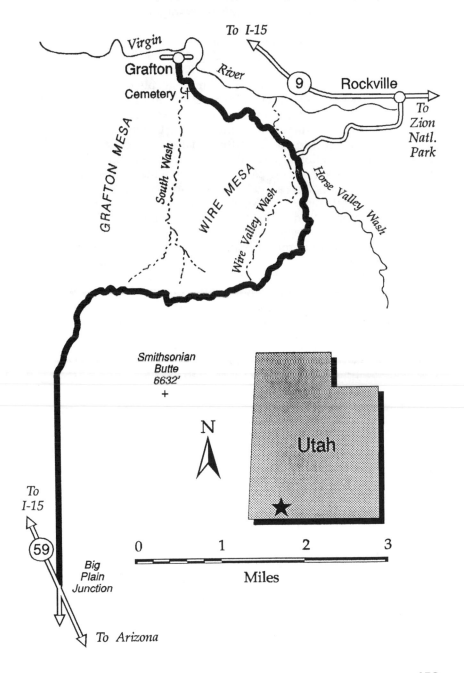

Virgin River

To I-15

Grafton

Cemetery †

9 Rockville

To Zion Natl. Park

GRAFTON MESA

South Wash

WIRE MESA

Wire Valley Wash

Horse Valley Wash

Smithsonian Butte 6632'
+

N

Utah

To I-15

59

Big Plain Junction

To Arizona

0   1   2   3

Miles

hookup campgrounds. The nearby Canaan Mountain plateau is a popular backpacker campsite.

Services: Limited services in Rockville. Full services in Springdale, Hurricane, Virgin, and St. George.

Nearby attractions: Zion National Park, Canaan Mountain Scenic Area, Pine Valley Mountain Wilderness Area, Snow Canyon State Park, St. George, Coral Pink Sand Dunes and Scenic Backway, Cedar Breaks National Monument, Dixie National Forest, Pipe Springs National Monument, Bryce Canyon National Park, Gold Butte Back Country Byway, Utah Scenic Byways 9, 89, and 12.

For more information: BLM, Cedar City District Office, 176 East D.L. Sargent Drive, P.O. Box 724, Cedar City, UT 84720. (801) 586-2401.

The trip: This nine-mile-long byway climbs steeply out of the Valley of the Virgin River at Rockville, four miles west of Zion National Park in Utah's far southwestern corner. Its upper reaches offer panoramic views of Zion's gleaming buttresses, buttes, and temples. The byway, coupled with a two-mile spur to the ghost town of Grafton, makes an excellent short excursion for visitors to the national park. The road, with one mile of pavement and eight miles of graded dirt, is passable to two-wheel drive vehicles in good weather. The road is also a Utah Scenic Backway.

Smithsonian Butte Byway is open year-round. Summer visitors should expect hot temperatures, with daily highs between ninety and 100 degrees. Much of the area's annual precipitation falls in violent summer thunderstorms. Travelers should not attempt driving the byway after heavy rain. The road gets very muddy. Winter is generally pleasant, with daytime highs between forty and sixty degrees, and nights below freezing.

The byway begins on Bridge Road south of Utah Highway 9 in the quiet town of Rockville four miles west of Zion National Park's west entrance. The road crosses the Virgin River on the Old Rockville Bridge, a girder bridge built in 1926. Turning west, the byway follows the river valley, verdant with grassy pastures and orchards, shady cottonwoods, grazing cattle, and the fragrance of Russian olive trees. The dramatic white- and caramel-colored cliffs of 147,035-acre Zion National Park, one of Utah's most spectacular parklands, tower eastward over the byway. Zion Canyon, the park's centerpiece, is a 3,000-foot-deep, narrow canyon carved by the unimposing Virgin River as it slices through eight major rock formations, some as old as 200 million years.

After one mile, the pavement ends and the byway turns away from the bucolic farmland and heads across benches of river-deposited gravel. Another mile brings the traveler to a road junction. The byway continues left, but a right turn leads two miles to Grafton, an abandoned ghost town and movie set.

Just before reaching Grafton, look for the pioneer cemetery to the south. The dusty graves include three of early settlers killed by Indians in 1866. Grafton, settled by five Mormon families in 1866, was deserted by 1907. All that remains today are the hollow ruins of an adobe church, a two-story ranch house, and several crumbling log cabins. Grafton is best known as being a set for the movie "Butch Cassidy and the Sundance Kid." The house used in the film, however, burned down in 1988.

The byway bends south from the junction with the Grafton road and heads up Horse Valley Wash. A ribbon of water runs down the wash in spring or after thunderstorms. The towering formations of the BLM's 50,000-acre

Spectacular rock peaks in Zion National Park tower over Virgin River Valley and the Smithsonian Butte Byway.

Canaan Mountain Scenic Area appear to the east. The broken cliffs of Eagle Crags, the 2,000-foot-high headwall of The Pines, and the Vermillion Cliffs also rise over the rocky canyon. The road climbs for a half-mile up a steep 10% grade to Wire Mesa. As it ascends, the byway passes through the colorful redbeds of Moenkopi and Chinle sandstone. Atop the mesa, the road levels out on a wide bench of resistant Kayenta sandstone.

At the top of the highest rise, a pullout gives marvelous views northeast into Zion Canyon. The panorama of rock formations includes West and East Temple, North Guardian Angel, and The Watchman. The large 6,632-foot-high block of Smithsonian Butte, its sharp cliffs seamed by gullies, dominates the southern sky above the byway.

Dutton Pass, made famous by W.H. Holmes 1872 illustrations of the area for the Powell Survey, connects Smithsonian Butte with Canaan Mountain. Captain Clarence Dutton was impressed by the view from the pass in 1877 when he wrote: "In an instant, there flashed before us a scene never to be forgotten. In coming time it will, I believe, take rank with a very small number of spectacles, each of which will, in its own way, be regarded as the most exquisite of its kind which the world discloses." Earlier, Major John Wesley Powell named the Vermillion Cliffs and Smithsonian Butte.

The byway winds along the wide benchland below Smithsonian Butte, flanked by a thick pinyon pine and juniper woodland. Wildflowers spread patches of color across the sandy soil in spring, including Indian paintbrush, beavertail cactus, penstemon, and Apache plume. Animal species inhabiting the area are mule deer, mountain lion, desert bighorn, hawks, golden eagles, roadrunners, kangaroo rats, collared lizards, and rattlesnakes.

The road slowly swings west around the butte's ragged escarpment before flattening out on the Big Plain. After a couple miles, the byway ends at Utah Highway 59. Hurricane lies fourteen miles west, while the Arizona border is eight miles east. Visitors staying in Zion National Park will probably want to retrace the byway back to Rockville. The returning views are just as spectacular.

35 NINE MILE CANYON
Utah

General description: A Type I, seventy-eight mile road through a scenic sandstone canyon and over high plateaus between Wellington and Myton in central Utah.

Special attractions: Indian petroglyphs and pictographs, Indian ruins, historic cabins, hiking, primitive camping, birdwatching, wildlife observation.

Location: Central Utah, east of Price. The byway leaves U.S. 191/U.S. 6 nine miles east of Price and two miles east of Wellington. The byway's northern access is two miles west of Myton on U.S. 40.

Byway route names: Soldier Creek Road, Nine-Mile Canyon Road, and Wells Draw Road.

Travel season: Year-round, although snow and mud can make the byway impassable in winter and early spring.

Camping: Primitive camping on BLM land along the byway. Pick up a BLM map in Price to make sure you're not camping on private land.

Services: All services in Wellington and Price.

Nearby attractions: Price, College of Eastern Utah Museum, Western Mining and Railroad Museum, Price Canyon Recreation Area, Cleveland Lloyd Dinosaur Quarry, San Rafael Swell, Desolation Canyon on the Green River, Ashley National Forest, Dinosaur National Monument, High Uintas Wilderness Area.

For more information: BLM, Moab District Office, 82 East Dogwood, P.O. Box 970, Moab, UT 84532. (801) 259-6111. BLM, Price River Resource Area, 900 North 700 East, Price, UT 84501. (801) 637-4584.

The trip: The Nine Mile Canyon Back Country Byway climbs over the Book and Roan Cliffs and winds along the floor of a spectacular sandstone canyon past galleries of rock art left by Indian artists over 1,000 years ago. The canyon is one of the Southwest's premier locations for rock art. The byway turns north up Gate Canyon from Nine Mile Canyon, and follows Wells Draw down to U.S. 40 near Myton. The byway follows the historic Price to Myton Road built by the U.S. Army's 9th Cavalry in 1886.

The Type I route is paved for its first twelve miles and graded gravel and dirt for the remainder. Plenty of pullouts along the byway allow for stops to view archeological and historical sites. The road is passable in good weather to passenger cars, however, several dry wash crossings in the canyon may be impassable after heavy rain. Recreation vehicles over twenty-two feet or trailers should not drive the route. The road is also a Utah State Scenic Backway. A handy brochure detailing Nine Mile Canyon's archaeology with road stops is available from the Utah Travel Council. Allow five or six hours to tour the byway and stop and view petroglyphs.

Summer is dry and warm, with daily highs between eighty and 100 degrees. Expect afternoon thunderstorms in July and August. Carry plenty of drinking water. Spring and fall are great times to explore the byway, with warm days and cool nights. Winter high temperatures are between thirty and fifty degrees. Snow and mud on the byway's upper elevations may close the road or require the use of a four-wheel-drive vehicle.

The byway begins on Soldier Creek Road off U.S. Highway 191/6 two miles east of Wellington. The paved road runs north through a shallow valley flanked by low scrubby hills covered with saltbush and juniper. Soldier Creek, its banks shaded by cottonwoods, meanders alongside the roadway. After almost eleven miles, the byway enters Soldier Creek Canyon, which cuts into one of Utah's many remarkable geologic features—the Book Cliffs and the Roan Cliffs.

The cliffs form an almost continuous wall that runs from north of Price to Grand Junction in western Colorado. Mancos shale and Mesa Verde sandstone, over seventy million years old, compose the lower Book Cliffs. The grey Mancos shale was deposited in a stagnant, oxygen-starved sea. The buff-colored, cliff-forming Mesa Verde sandstone caps the soft shale. The Wasatch Formation, a 2,000-foot-thick, strawberry-colored sandstone, forms the Roan Cliffs above the byway's upper reaches.

Two miles up Soldier Creek Canyon, the pavement ends at a coal mine. The dirt road continues up a steep-walled canyon, past sandstone bands and through a pinyon pine and juniper forest. Beyond the canyon, it enters Whitmore Park, a rolling sagebrush-covered valley between the Book Cliffs and the Roan Cliffs. Old homesteads and corrals dot the high valley. The road swings northeast around Minnie Maud Ridge and crosses a 7,300-foot summit, the byway's high point. Forests of pine, fir, and aspen spill down moist north-facing slopes east of the road. From the summit, the byway descends into Nine Mile Canyon.

An old homestead, now the haunt of lizards, bats, and sheep, lies along the byway just past the bridge over Minnie Maud Creek in the canyon bottom. Many of the historic settler cabins along the byway in Nine Mile Canyon date from the 1880s. A half-mile east sits a BLM sign that interprets the canyon. The canyon walls, stairstepped with bands of sandstone cliffs, are densely forested with pinyon pine, juniper, and scrub oak. Clumps of aspen and pine

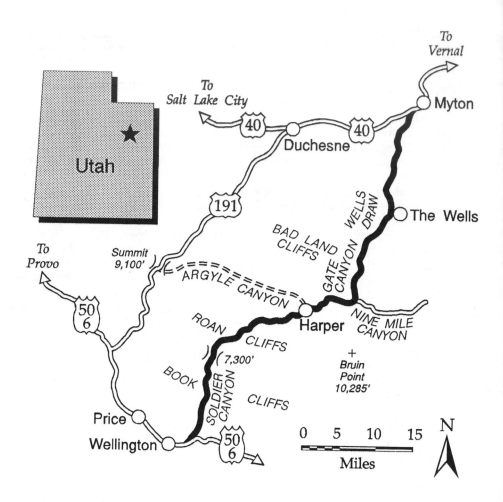

grow along the rimrock. Minnie Maud Creek, a perennial stream, is bordered by shady cottonwoods and tamarisk thickets. Grassy hayfields and cattle pastures spread across the canyon floor. Much of the land along the creek is private property, respect the owner's rights.

A little over three miles east of the homestead lies the first major rock art panel. Two types of rock art are found in Nine Mile Canyon—petroglyphs and pictographs. Petroglyphs are designs pecked and incised onto the rock surface. They are usually found on cliff faces and boulders that are darker than the surrounding rock. Pictographs are designs painted on the rock surface with mineral and plant colors. They are quick to weather and are found mostly under sharp rock overhangs. Along the rest of the byway within Nine Mile Canyon are thousands of rock art panels. Keep a sharp lookout and you will sight many of the roadside galleries.

The art is a legacy left by many different peoples from as early as 6,000 years ago to historic times. Much of it was created by Indians of the Fremont culture that inhabited the canyon as early as 300 A.D. and left by 1100 A.D. These Indians were part-time farmers who grew corn, beans, and squash along the creek's flood plain. They roamed across central Utah chasing deer, bighorn sheep, and rabbits. They built semi-permanent homes and graneries in the cliffs. And they pecked and painted marvelous works of art using the sandstone walls as a canvas. Early ancestors of the Utes also contributed many examples of rock art.

Continuing east down the road the byway slowly loses elevation. The cliffs become higher and the canyon floor and sides drier. Near Argyle Canyon, the ghost town of Harper nestles among tall cottonwoods. This makes a good lunch stop. Harper was once a stage stop and post office. A road northwest up Argyle Canyon just east of Harper leads to U.S. Highway 191.

There are several stories about how a canyon over fifty miles long acquired the name Nine Mile Canyon. The most accurate says the name was given by the 1869 John Wesley Powell expedition that floated down the Green and Colorado rivers. The group's mapmaker used the mouth of Nine Mile Canyon on the Green River as a point for a nine-mile triangulation map of the area. The canyon was used as an Army supply road between Price and Fort Duchesne from the 1880s until the fort closed in 1912. Homesteaders, miners, and stagecoaches also used the canyon route.

At Gate Canyon, the byway turns north and twists up the narrow gorge for a couple miles. Cliffs and steep rocky slopes tower over the road. The original army route followed the wash, passing between sandstone walls. Midway up the canyon, a natural bridge once spanned the canyon floor and road. But fear that the bridge was decaying from the vibrations of rumbling stagecoaches and freight wagons led to its demise. The bridge was dynamited in 1905.

The canyon widens as the byway climbs up it, passing over wide sandstone benches, through the Bad Land Cliffs, and over a wide saddle. Before reaching the saddle, a one-and-a-half-mile trail strikes north, following the pre-1920 road build by the army. Rock walls, culverts, and road cuts still remain along the path. The trail ends on the north side of the divide.

The byway drops down into Wells Draw and follows it northeast through shallow rock-rimmed canyons and past sagebrush-filled plains. A few ruins beneath dry, sun-baked cliffs at The Wells testify to the bustle of the pioneer freight road. Owen Smith dug a 196-foot-deep well here in 1891 and established

Art galleries of ancient Anasazi petroglyphs line the Nine Mile Canyon Byway.

an overnight stopover. At its height it boasted a stage station, general store, feed yard, blacksmith shop, hotel, and restaurant. This was the only water stop on the forty-mile route between Myton and Nine Mile Canyon.

Beyond The Wells, the road continues along Wells Draw for about six miles before climbing out. Gilsonite, a solid form of oil used in industry, was mined in this area and freighted along the old road. The byway slowly drops down into the fertile Duchesne River valley, rolling over sagebrush hills, before crossing a couple canals and ending on U.S. 40 two miles west of Myton.

A good side trip begins in Nine Mile Canyon where the byway turns north up Gate Canyon. Continue east on the Nine Mile Canyon Road. The canyon deepens and becomes lined with towering sandstone cliffs. Grassy pastures and shady cottonwoods line Minnie Maud Creek. Many rock art panels and small cliff dwellings can be sighted from the road. A rough 1.5 mile drive up Cottonwood Canyon leads to an outstanding petroglyph panel of a hunting scene. The side trip ends after about eleven miles at a locked gate. Beyond lies private property and further down-canyon the Green River runs glassy through rocky Desolation Canyon.

When traveling along the Nine Mile Canyon Back Country Byway, remember that its archaeological and historical sites are protected by the Antiquities Act. Visitors may not "appropriate, excavate, injure, or destroy an historic or prehistoric ruin or monument, or any object of antiquity." Little is known now of the Fremont people. This canyon is like a closed book, waiting to be opened and studied by future archaeologists. Picking up an artifact, vandalizing its rock art, or disturbing a burial is not only plundering the past, but stealing from the future.

36   SOUTH BIGHORN / RED WALL
Wyoming

General description: A Type II, 101-mile-long byway through the high plains and foothills south of the Bighorn Mountains in central Wyoming.

Special attractions: Scenic vistas, wildlife, hiking, camping, Red Wall, South Bighorn Sheep Ranching Monument, Rough Lock, historic stock trail.

Location: Central Wyoming. The byway's eastern access, Natrona County Road 125, is thirteen miles east of Casper on U.S. 20/26. The western access, Natrona County 104, is at Waltman forty-eight miles west of Casper on U.S. 20/26.

Byway route numbers: Natrona County Roads 125, 110, 109, 105, and 104.

Travel season: May through November. Snow closes the upper section of the byway. The lower sections are often snowy and muddy in winter and spring.

Camping: Two primitive BLM campgrounds at Grave Springs and Buffalo Creek. Primitive camping is allowed on BLM lands along the byway.

Services: All services are available in Casper.

Nearby attractions: Casper, Fort Casper, Seminoe to Alcova Back Country Byway, Edness Kimball Wilkins State Park, Hell's Half Acre, Oregon Trail, Bighorn National Forest, Middle Fork BLM Recreation Area.

For more information: BLM, Casper District Office, 1701 East E Street, Casper, WY 82601. (307) 261-7600.

The trip: The South Bighorn-Red Wall Back Country Byway travels over the rolling plains northwest of Casper and into the scenic foothills of the southern Bighorn Mountains. The Type II byway, with both paved and gravel segments, is passable to high-clearance, two-wheel-drive vehicles. Passenger cars can negotiate the byway, except for the upper section that climbs to the sheep monument. This can be avoided by following Buffalo Creek on Natrona County Road 105.

Elevations on the byway range from 5,430 feet to over 8,800 feet. Summer and fall are the best times to drive the route. Expect daily temperatures in

The South Bighorn/Red Wall Byway drops down into Buffalo Creek's broad valley.

summer to exceed ninety degrees. September and October highs are usually between sixty and eighty degrees, although highs can be in the thirties. It is often windy. Strong winds funnel through the byway region from the Wind River Basin to the west. Winters are generally dry but very cold. Snow blocks the byway's upper elevations from November through April. Watch for mud on the byway from snowmelt and after heavy thunderstorms. Like all the byways, be prepared for emergencies by carrying adequate food, water, and gas. About five hours is needed to drive the route.

The byway begins off U.S. 20/26 almost fifteen miles west of Casper. Turn north on paved Natrona County Road 125. The road heads north, slowly climbing onto a high, rolling plain, cut with shallow arroyos, carpeted with grass and sagebrush, and grazed by herds of fleet pronghorn antelope. After five

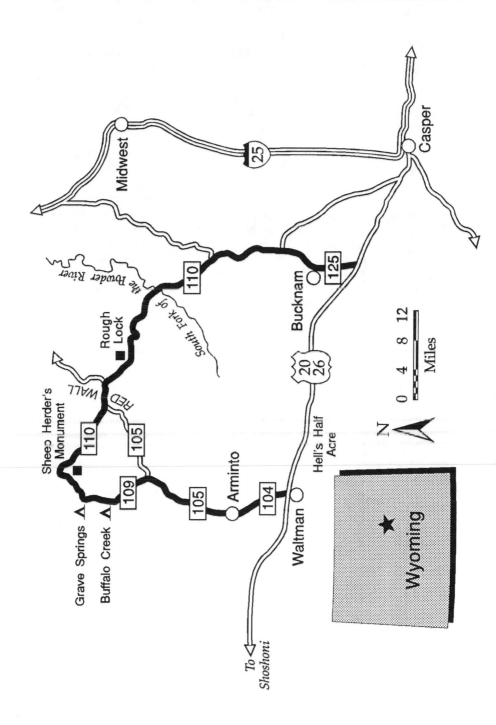

163

miles the byway crosses Casper Creek and railroad tracks, and passes Bucknum, a railroad siding.

The road continues north over sand hills stabilized with grass and sagebrush. These dunes, deposited by persistent westerly winds, are part of a long belt of dormant sand dunes that reach from Shoshoni to east of Casper. The dunes, now vegetated, formed after the retreat of glaciers in the Wind River Mountains between 12,000 and 19,000 years ago.

This byway section follows the 33-Mile/Arminto Stock Trail, a pioneer stock driveway that still allows ranchers to drive cattle and sheep to summer pastures in the southern Bighorns in May and June and back to winter ranges in late fall.

After nine miles the byway becomes Natrona County Road 110. The road rolls over the undulating plain. Dramatic views unfold. To the north tower the lofty Bighorn Mountains, snow glistening in their alpine cirques. Casper Mountain spreads its long forested ridge above the North Platte valley to the south. The pavement ends after twenty-one miles, and the road becomes graded gravel. After another nine miles the byway crosses the South Fork of the Powder River, dipping down into its deeply carved arroyo. Bands of white alkali and occasional willows and tamarisk line the river's meager flow. The road climbs out the other side onto a wide bench called Fifty-Mile Flat that is plowed and reseeded for grazing.

The byway climbs west away from the wide Powder River Valley and passes through tilted sandstone layers in an anticline. Ponderosa pine and juniper grow along the ridgelines, and grassy meadows and cattails line pools of water in shallow canyons. On the anticline's west side, the road splits a gap surrounded by rosy sandstone cliffs. A small window sits north of the byway.

Continuing west, the road dips and rises through steep canyons lined with ponderosa pines, small crags, and shale badlands. Between canyons it crosses wide, barren benches with distant views of the Bighorns. The byway splashes through Alkali Creek in the bottom of a deep arroyo and then climbs up bare shale slopes into a region of upthrust sedimentary strata.

The road parallels a steep escarpment that drops abruptly to the north. A small BLM sign alongside the road marks Rough Lock. Walk north from today's jeep road to a gap facing northwest. Here pioneers locked their wagon wheels with thick branches and skidded down the steep rocky slope to the basin below. Their slipping wheels scarred the hillside, leaving a deep swale. Today, the wagon tracks sweep around a prominent headland and head north toward the old Bridger Trail and the Montana mine fields.

Past Rough Lock, the byway drops down a strike valley between hogbacks and follows a shelf road down a cliffed face to Buffalo Creek. The Red Wall, one of central Wyoming's most distinctive geographic features, forms a forty-five-mile-long escarpment that borders Buffalo Creek on the east. North of here is the Hole-in-the-Wall and Outlaw Cave, the temporary hideout of the infamous Hole-in-the-Wall gang led by Butch Cassidy and the Sundance Kid.

The byway turns on the west side of Buffalo Creek and begins climbing steeply up a wide ridge flanked by deep white sandstone canyons. Pine and juniper fill the moist canyons. After a rough, rocky twelve miles, the road reaches the top of the byway and the pyramid-shaped South Bighorn Sheep Ranching Monument. The monument honors the area's pioneer sheepmen. These upper elevations are well-watered, with grassy meadows and stands of lodgepole pine. Mule deer and elk often graze these high pastures.

Turn south at the monument on Natrona County 109 and head southwest.

The Red Wall, a long sandstone escarpment, borders the South Bighorn/Red Wall Byway.

The byway rises and falls over several high ridges, passing two BLM recreation sites—Grave Springs and Buffalo Creek. Both are cool spots in summer. Facilities include campgrounds, picnic areas, and restrooms. Past the Buffalo Creek site, the byway climbs a ridge then descends down South Buffalo Creek to the Red Wall.

This twenty-six-mile byway loop section is generally passable only to high-clearance vehicles. Passenger cars can avoid it by following Natrona County Road 105 along Buffalo Creek for about twelve miles. This road section, in the shadow of the Red Wall, is also scenic.

After rejoining Natrona County 105, the byway runs south alongside the towering Red Wall and across dusty red washes and badlands. Deadman Butte, a prominent landmark rimmed with cliffs, sits alongside the byway near the end of the Red Wall. Beyond, the road swings away from the wall and climbs through a shale ridge into a wide, dry basin that stretches south to the Rattlesnake Range.

The byway becomes paved just before Arminto, crosses the railroad tracks, and climbs onto a grassy ridge. A grey badlands, cut into the ridge flank, lies east of the road. The byway rolls south over rounded hills and ends eight miles south of Arminto at Waltman on U.S. 20/26.

Casper is forty-eight miles to the southeast. Hell's Half Acre sits a few miles east of Waltman. This unusual area, a Natrona County park, looks like a miniature Grand Canyon with dramatically eroded fins, spires, cliffs, hoodoos, and goblins. It's good for hiking and exploration. Shoshoni is forty-nine miles west of Waltman on U.S. 20/26.

General description: This thirty-two-mile-long, Type II byway traverses colorful badlands, canyons, and high ridges through the western foothills of the Bighorn Mountains in north-central Wyoming.

Special attractions: Primitive camping, hiking, photography, wildlife, picnicking, scenic views, rockhounding, hunting.

Location: North-central Wyoming. The byway's northern access is on U.S. 14, four miles west of Shell and ten miles east of Greybull. Turn south on the Red Gulch/Alkali Road. The southern access is on Wyoming State Highway 31, just north of Hyattville. Turn north on the Alkali/Cold Springs Road, then left on Alkali Road.

Byway route names: Red Gulch Road, Alkali Road.

Travel season: May through mid-October. Snow and mud closes the byway during winter and spring. The road is impassable in wet weather.

Camping: Primitive camping is allowed on BLM land along the byway. A campground is near Medicine Lodge State Archeological Site. Many campgrounds abound in nearby Bighorn National Forest.

Services: All services are available in Greybull and Shell. Limited services in Hyattville.

Nearby attractions: Medicine Lodge State Archaeological Site, Alkali Creek WSA, Medicine Lodge Creek WSA, Trapper Creek WSA, Bighorn National Forest, Cloud Peak Wilderness Area, Cloud Peak Skyway Scenic Byway, Bighorn Scenic Byway, Shell Creek Falls, Bighorn Canyon National Recreation Area, Medicine Wheel National Historic Landmark.

For more information: BLM, Worland District, 101 South 23 Street, Worland, WY 82401. (307) 347-9871.

The trip: The thirty-two-mile Red Gulch/Alkali Back Country Byway meanders through scenic foothills on the western edge of Wyoming's lofty Bighorn Mountains. The road, passing over remote BLM lands, offers solitude, an array of recreational opportunities, and spectacular views across the vast Bighorn Basin.

The Type II, unpaved byway is easily driven in a high-clearance vehicle, and, conditions permitting, in a passenger car. The road is narrow with occasional pullouts, but other traffic is rare. The road, passing over clay and shale, is impassable when wet after thunderstorms and from snowmelt in springtime. Allow two or three hours to drive the byway.

Weather in this semiarid region is hot in summer and cold in winter. Summer high temperatures are between eighty and 100 degrees. Expect breezy afternoons and occasional thunderstorms. Autumns are cooler, with highs ranging from fifty to eighty degrees. Snow can fall anytime after mid-September and usually closes the byway in October.

The byway begins on U.S. Highway 14, about ten miles east of Greybull and four miles west of Shell, on the south edge of Shell Creek's broad valley. Turn south on Red Gulch Road. Ranches, pastures, and hayfields border U.S. 14 as it heads eastward to Shell Canyon in the Bighorn Mountains. The Bighorn Scenic Byway begins in Shell.

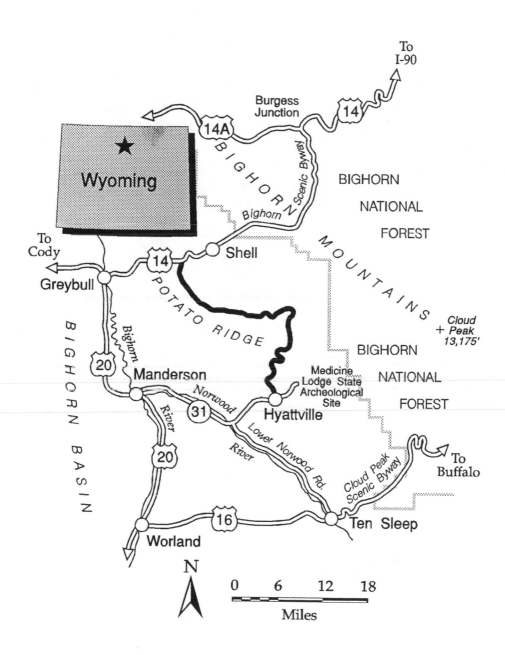

Wyoming

To
I-90

Burgess
Junction

14A

14

BIGHORN

NATIONAL

FOREST

B I G H O R N

Scenic Byway

Bighorn

To
Cody

14

Shell

Greybull

P O T A T O   R I D G E

M O U N T A I N S

Cloud
Peak
13,175'

BIGHORN

NATIONAL

FOREST

Bighorn

20

Manderson

Norwood

31

Hyattville

Medicine
Lodge State
Archeological
Site

B I G H O R N   B A S I N

River

20

River

Lower Norwood Rd.

Cloud Peak
Scenic Byway

To
Buffalo

16

Ten Sleep

Worland

N

0   6   12   18

Miles

The road enters a region of dry, rolling hills, sparsely covered with sagebrush, saltbush, and scattered sandstone outcrops. A mile south it traverses bare shale ridges, encrusted with white alkali. All around are eroded badlands. East of the foothills and the byway looms the long western escarpment of the Bighorn Mountains, a towering wall that culminates in snowcapped 13,167-foot Cloud Peak.

The Red Gulch/Alkali byway follows a geologic transition zone between the Bighorn Mountains uplift on the east and the syncline or downwarp of the Bighorn Basin to the west. The road, as it heads south, crosses over the tops of eroded hogbacks of folded Mesozoic sandstone and shale strata that were thrust-faulted westward over the basin. The byway passes through the distinctive Chugwater Formation, a brilliant red sandstone, in both its first few miles and in the canyons just north of Hyattville. The Chugwater was deposited 230 million years ago in a warm shallow sea that inundated Wyoming.

Climbing steadily, the byway snakes up the grass- and sagebrush-covered flank of a high plateau that bulges west from the mountains. The higher the road ascends, the more spectacular the view. Snowfields on the Absaroka Mountains, over seventy miles to the west, gleam over the vast Bighorn Basin. Three Wilderness Study Areas—Trapper Creek, Alkali Creek, and Medicine Lodge Creek—adjoin the byway.

Much wildlife roams over this wild, upland region, including elk, mule deer, bighorn sheep, black bear, mountain lion, and coyote. Game birds are chukar, sage and blue grouse, pheasant, and wild turkey. Raptors include not only hawks and owls, but both golden and bald eagles.

The Red Gulch/Alkaki Byway winds through the western foothills of the Bighorn Mountains.

After twelve miles the road climbs atop the plateau and winds east toward the mountains along the plateau's edge. Evidence of sheep and cattle grazing that dates back to the 1880s lies along the byway here, including fences, wells, holding pens, and small reservoirs. Livestock still graze this land on their way to summer pastures in the Bighorns or winter pastures in the basin below. Piles of carefully stacked rock or cairns dot ridges along the byway. These "sheep herder monuments," some as old as 100 years, were made by sheepmen as landmarks or out of boredom.

Red Gulch Road joins Alkali Road after twenty miles of climbing. This lonely junction is the road's high point. The Bighorn National Forest boundary lies ten miles east on Red Gulch Road from here. Turning south the byway drops quickly down a wide ridge. Four miles down on the east is a pretty canyon chiseled out of sandstone, with low cliffs, spires, and rimrock.

The byway swings down steep ridges into a wide valley carved through a hogback of red Chugwater sandstone. Buttes and rolling hills surround the byway as it heads south. Spectacular canyons seam the high plateau to the east. The road passes several ranches, and ends on Wyoming Highway 31 north of Hyattville.

Medicine Lodge State Archaeological Site lies a few miles east of the byway on Cold Springs Road, a left turn just before the byway's end. This important archaeological and historical site was home for thousands of years to Indians that settled on the sheltered banks of Medicine Lodge Creek on the Bighorns' western flank. Ancient tools, artifacts, and fossils have been unearthed here. Rock art, petroglyphs and pictographs, decorate area cliffs. Facilities include a small visitor center, campground, and several scenic hiking trails.

38 SEMINOE to ALCOVA
Wyoming

General description: A Type I, sixty-four-mile byway that crosses wide basins, passes Seminoe and Alcova Reservoirs, and traverses the rugged Seminoe Mountains in south-central Wyoming.

Special attractions: Scenic views, picnicking, hiking, camping, fishing, rock climbing, Miracle Mile, North Platte River, Seminoe State Park, Alcova Reservoir, wildlife.

Location: South-central Wyoming. The byway's southern access is at Sinclair, six miles west of Rawlins on Interstate 80. Take either Sinclair exit and turn north on Carbon County Road 351, following signs toward Seminoe State Park. The northern access is at Alcova on Wyoming Highway 220 about thirty miles southwest of Casper. Head south on Natrona County Road 408.

Byway route numbers: Carbon County 351, Natrona County 407 and 408.

Travel season: May through November. Heavy snow generally makes the byway impassable over the Seminoe Mountains from December through April.

Camping: Seminoe State Park has forty-seven campsites in two campgrounds. Camping is also available at Alcova Reservoir and Alcova. Primitive camping is possible on BLM lands along the byway.

The Seminoe to Alcova Byway drops down from the crest of the Seminoe Range to the North Platte River.

Services: All services are available in Rawlins, Sinclair, Alcova, and Casper.
Nearby attractions: Casper, Fort Casper, South Bighorn/Red Wall Back Country Byway, Pathfinder Reservoir, Pathfinder National Wildlife Refuge, Fremont Canyon, Independence Rock, Devil's Gate, Oregon Trail, Medicine Bow National Forest, Trapper Route Canoe Trail, Grey Reef Reservoir, Fort Steele Historic Site.
For more information: BLM, Rawlins District, 1300 N. Third Street, Rawlins, WY 82301. (307) 324-7171.

The trip: The Type I Seminoe to Alcova Back Country Byway travels across lonely basins and mountains in south-central Wyoming. A wealth of recrea-

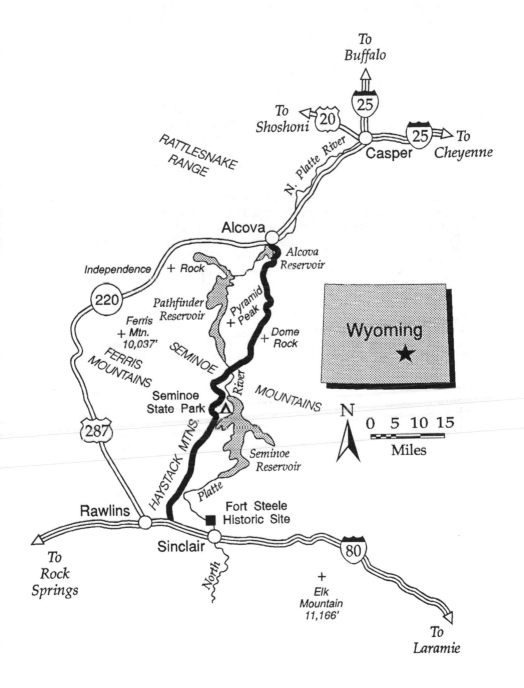

To
Buffalo

To
Shoshoni

25

20

25

To
Cheyenne

Casper

RATTLESNAKE
RANGE

N. Platte River

Alcova

Alcova
Reservoir

Independence

+ Rock

Wyoming

220

Pathfinder
Reservoir

Pyramid
+ Peak

Ferris
+ Mtn.
10,037'

FERRIS
MOUNTAINS

SEMINOE

+ Dome
Rock

287

Seminoe
State Park

River

MOUNTAINS

N

0 5 10 15

Miles

Seminoe
Reservoir

HAYSTACK MTNS.

Platte

Rawlins

Fort Steele
Historic Site

To
Rock
Springs

Sinclair

North

80

+

Elk
Mountain
11,166'

To
Laramie

tional opportunities, including camping, excellent fishing, hiking, boating, and wildlife study, are found along the byway.

The byway varies from paved, two-lane road on the north and south to a narrow, gravel segment in the mountains. Numerous pullouts along the byway allow for scenic views and passing. The byway, open from May through November is easily passable in a passenger car. Heavy snows in winter close the road, although four-wheel-drives with chains may make it over the Seminoe Mountains. Motorhomes and vehicles pulling trailers are discouraged from driving the byway between Seminoe Reservoir and the Miracle Mile because of steep mountain grades.

The weather along the byway during summer and fall is generally mild. Expect summer temperatures in the lower basins to exceed ninety degrees. It's cooler atop the mountains. Gusty afternoon winds blow almost every day throughout the travel season. Winters are cold and windy, with snow closing the byway's upper section over the Seminoe Mountains.

The byway begins in Sinclair, six miles east of Rawlins on Interstate 80. Take either Sinclair exit, turn north on Carbon County Road 351, and follow signs to Seminoe State Park. The town of Sinclair was originally named Parco, short for Producers and Refiners Corporation, the first owners of the refinery. After Sinclair Oil Company acquired the refinery in 1934, the town was renamed for its new owner. Today, it's Wyoming's largest oil refinery.

The road heads north from Sinclair across a high, dry basin that is rimmed on the east by the Haystack Mountains, part of the Fort Steele anticline. To the south lies 11,166-foot Elk Mountain, the northern outpost of the Medicine Bow Mountains, lifting its dark forested ridges skyward. The byway runs north and then east toward the Haystacks, passing scrubby sagebrush and saltbush on the basin floor.

After almost seven miles the road leaves the basin and climbs through upturned sandstone layers. It then turns abruptly south and drops down a strike valley to meet up with the North Platte River. The North Platte, one of Wyoming's principal rivers, originates below the Continental Divide in Colorado's North Park and runs 618 miles through Wyoming and Nebraska to its confluence with the South Platte. The BLM Dugway Recreation Site, with camping, picnicking, fishing, and boating, lies just south of the byway where it meets the river.

The byway follows the river, lined with tamarisk, willow, and cottonwood, as it slices a three-mile-long canyon through the Haystack Mountains. Bands of tilted sandstone cliffs, patches of gray sagebrush, and small junipers scatter across the steep canyon slopes.

Beyond the canyon, the byway swings north away from the river and parallels the Haystacks. Magnificent views abound. To the east lies a wide basin, covered with sagebrush and short grass and broken by sandy hills and gravel ridges. The North Platte meanders through a shallow rock canyon across the basin to eighteen-mile-long Seminoe Reservoir.

Ragged mountain ranges—the Seminoe and the Ferris mountains—fill the northern horizon. The wild Ferris Mountains are marked by a prominent limestone cliff band that marches along the range's southwestern flank. Ferris Peak, at 10,037 feet, is the range's high point. The Seminoe Mountains form a high, jagged wall cleaved by deep canyons, tilted sandstone slabs, and craggy summits. Bradley Peak, the range apex at 8,948 feet, towers northwest of the byway.

As the byway swings northeast below the Seminoe Mountains, the road dips and climbs over rounded hogbacks and shallow valleys. The reservoir spreads over the basin floor to the east. White sand along the lake edge forms swimming beaches. The region lies across the Killpecker Sand Dunes, an inactive, mostly vegetabed dune belt that reaches from Wyoming into Nebraska. Blowing snad here has deposited small dunes in the shallow valley bottoms below the mountains. The byway swings around one large dune. Water, trapped by the sand, forms unusual lakes nestled among the dune.

Further on the byway passes steep, rock-rimmed hogbacks and the entrance to Sunshine Beach. After almost thirty-one miles, the pavement ends and the byway becomes a two-lane, gravel road. Just past here are the South Red Hills and North Red Hills entrances to Seminoe State Park. Both have campsites, picnic areas, boat ramps, and restrooms.

The byway switchbacks u the side of the Seminoe Mountains to a lofty overlook of the reservoir and surrounding landscape. The lake below, now tucked into a narrow mountain canyon, is surrounded by high cliffs, sharp aretes, and forested slopes. The Bennett Mountains, an extension of the Seminoes, edges off to the southeast. A half-mile further on is the Seminoe Dam Overlook and an interpretative sign.

The road winds through the rugged Seminoe Mountains, following steep-walled canyons lined with ponderosa pine and sharp granite outcrops. Aspen groves, willows, and cottonwoods line the creekbeds. About six miles from the first overlook, the byway reaches a high divide and then drops abruptly down a steep canyon, past soaring rock ribs. Beyond, the byway leaves the canyon and empties onto an outwash plain on the western edge of a wide basin.

The byway crosses the North Platte River as it meanders northward to Pathfinder Reservoir. This river section, the Miracle Mile, is renowned as a blue ribbon trout fishery. A parking area for fishermen is just south of the river bridge. Pathfinder Reservoir and Pathfinder National Wildlife Refuge lie to the north. The lake and refuge are an important feeding and nesting area for waterfowl. A breeding colony of white pelicans live on a lake island.

Most of the land the byway traverses is remote and unpopulated, and is great wildlife habitat. Visitors often sight pronghorn antelope and mule deer along the road; more rarely seen are elk and bighorn sheep. Other mammals living here include mountain lion, bobcat, coyote, fox, skunk, porcupine, racoon, and beaver. Raptors—hawks and eagles—often soar overhead. Reptiles include bull snakes and prairie rattlesnakes.

Past the river, the byway crosses the rolling basin, passing rough ridges of smooth granite and wide sagebrush-covered plains. The road drops into the shallow valley of Sage Creek and climbs up a slope beyond to the Pedro Mountains. The Pedros, a sharp, granite range, are sparsely forested with ponderosa pine and juniper. Dome Rock, a smooth dome broken by cracks and buttresses, looms east of the byway.

The road runs north over a tawny plain before dropping down to Alcova Reservoir. Distant mountain ranges to the west gleam in the hazy light, their spiked ridges piercing the skyline. The reservoir is surrounded by badlands, sagebrush flats, upturned sandstone hogbacks, and juniper forests. The road swings around the lake's south side, passing several spur roads to the shore. It bends around the dam, crosses the North Platte River below the spillway, and enters the town of Alcova and the byway's end on Wyoming

Highway 220. Casper lies thirty miles to the northeast. Independence Rock, a famed Oregon Trail landmark, lies about twenty-five miles to the southwest.

Mule deer are a common sight along the Seminoe to Alcova Byway.